Ways of Doing

CAMBRIDGE HANDBOOKS FOR LANGUAGE TEACHERS

This is a series of practical guides for teachers of English and other languages. Illustrative examples are usually drawn from the field of English as a foreign or second language, but the ideas and techniques described can equally well be used in the teaching of any language.

Ways of Doing

Students explore their everyday
and classroom processes

Paul Davis
Barbara Garside
Mario Rinvolucri

CAMBRIDGE
UNIVERSITY PRESS

PUBLISHED BY THE PRESS SYNDICATE OF THE UNIVERSITY OF CAMBRIDGE
The Pitt Building, Trumpington Street, Cambridge CB2 1RP, United Kingdom

CAMBRIDGE UNIVERSITY PRESS
The Edinburgh Building, Cambridge CB2 2RU, United Kingdom
40 West 20th Street, New York, NY 10011–4211, USA
10 Stamford Road, Oakleigh, Melbourne 3166, Australia

First published 1998

Printed in the United Kingdom at the University Press, Cambridge

Typeset in Sabon 10.5/12pt

A catalogue record for this book is available
from the British Library

Library of Congress Cataloguing in Publication data

Davis, Paul, 1952–
    Ways of doing : students explore their everyday and classroom
processes / Paul Davis, Barbara Garside, Mario Rinvolucri.
        p. cm. — (Cambridge handbooks for language teachers)
    Includes bibliographical references.
    ISBN 0–521–58559–7 (pbk.)
        1. Language and languages—Study and teaching.   2. Learning.
I. Garside, Barbara.   II. Rinvolucri, Mario.   III. Title.
IV. Series.
P53.D33   1998
418'.007—dc21   98–44353
                                                                      CIP

ISBN 0 521 58559 7 paperback

Contents

Contents

Thanks and acknowledgements

We would like to thank language students and teachers on training courses at Pilgrims, Canterbury, UK, in Cambridge, UK and in Izmir, Turkey, for having helped us try out and develop the ideas in this book.

We also owe a debt of gratitude to the teachers whom Cambridge University Press invited to pilot parts of the book. This gave us a perspective from outside our own narrow experience.

Thanks go to Penny Ur, our series editor, who tightened the book up and helped us to make it more relevant to secondary school classes of 50 students. She kept reminding us to think beyond our own classes.

We would like to thank John Morgan who pulled the manuscript into shape and implemented or modified Penny's editorial recommendations. He gave the authors support at a time when we needed it. Thank you, John. We would also like to thank Jenny Daniels, not only for her word-processing skills but also for her valuable input and encouragement. Finally, we would like to thank Lola Rinvolucri for re-keying the whole manuscript.

Introduction

What interests you as your eye lights on this page? If you want to find out how we feel this book fits into mainstream EFL thinking, then please read section A of this introduction **Where in language teaching?**

If you would like our thoughts on how the book fits into the progression of humanistic teaching then please read section B **Where in the humanistic tradition?**

If you want an outline of the sorts of practical benefits the exercises in the book will bring to your students and to you, then read section C **Benefits.**

If you want a tour of the book's contents and some of its features then read section D **What's where?**

A Where in language teaching?

In the late eighties EFL teachers began to notice 'Action Research' (A.R.), a movement in general education in which classroom teachers looked into what was going on in their own classrooms. The A.R. movement in EFL came as a reaction against the assumption that classroom research was the exclusive domain of the university. It was as if a generation of guinea pigs decided to put on white coats

and look at their behaviours and beliefs themselves. The proponents of A.R. suggest that a teacher first formulates a hypothesis about some aspect of what is going on in their classroom; and then collects data relevant to the hypothesis. They evaluate the data and either formulate a new hypothesis or decide on some action they will take in the light of the data. The Action Research practitioner intends it to be a dynamic element in their teaching process. In the hands of pioneers like Melanie Ellis in Poland and Graziella Pozzo in Italy, it is just that.

In a simpler model of A.R., the teacher identifies some area of their own practice that they want to find out more about. The teacher then collects data from their classroom and, in the light of the data, decides how to improve things.

While A.R. wrests power from the hands of the professional gatekeepers (the university caste) and places it in the hands of the teachers, our book goes one step further: it puts this power of self-research into the hands of the students. In using this book with your students, you will be giving them instruments for finding out a lot more about themselves as people, as learners, as foreign-language learners and as members of a group.

The methodology we use to facilitate this student self-discovery does not go along with the hypothesis → data-collection → evaluation model favoured in some A.R., which is perhaps not the most elegant of scientific models to borrow. We have found it more flexible to borrow the 'field study' approach prevalent in a scientific area like geology. Put in simple terms, we ask the student to observe acutely what is there, to direct close attention to areas they have previously given no thought to. The realisations thus arrived at give the student a whole new 'mapping' of the area under consideration. The new mapping may lead to new and different courses of action.

An example of the field study type of methodology as we use it in this book is appropriate here:

1 The group sits in a circle so they can all see each other.

2 Anybody may pick up the ball placed in the centre of the circle, and throw it to another group member who reminds them of somebody from elsewhere in their life. They then explain the resemblance: 'You look / sound / feel to me like X because ...' They also begin to deal with the projection by adding:
'But you are different from X because ...'

This exercise (which you will find laid out in greater detail on page 116 of *Grammar in Action Again*, Frank and Rinvolucri) offers the learner group a first step into the area of projections, those distorting mirrors that dynamically affect life in the classroom. When students discover for themselves that a fair number of people in the group harbour mild to strong projections on other students that they are able to speak about (forget about the ones they are too ashamed of to speak about), the way they belong to the group is immediately modified. The new mapping of the group that each person gets is dynamic knowledge and over the following days will modify the way the individual relates to other group members.

We believe that awarenesses that suddenly burst into a person's consciousness lead directly to attitudinal and behavioural changes. If you get a detailed representation of your own daydreaming process (p.14), in class or elsewhere, you have the option of changing the pattern. It is possible you will never daydream fully 'innocently' again.

Not learner training

Our book suggests to the students possibilities for finding out about their ways of doing things and avoids any suggestion of what is good for them. This book is a small step towards getting students to chart their own mental processes, their schemata, their representational systems, and so help build up a new body of professional knowledge, researched by the students themselves. We feel that it is useful to help students to find out some of the marvellous ways they *do* learn rather than proposing ways they might learn more effectively.

Teacher development

Section 7 in this book (**Teacher to teacher**) stands away from the rest of the text in that it deals with teacher rather than student process. In our view the exercises in this section are ideal for a teacher development group rather than a teacher training one.

You may reasonably wonder what the differences between a TD and a TT group are. We feel the political/power differences are significant and these have direct repercussions on openness to new ideas and ability to learn.

In a classical teacher development group (as opposed to a teacher training group):

- people meet in their own time, not paid time
- people may leave or join the group of their own free will
- the agenda belongs uniquely to the group
- the meetings are not run by an outside authority/expert
- people take full responsibility for what does or does not happen

Maybe the main difference between TD and TT centres round the question of ownership. A thoughtful colleague at a small school in Cambridge said this in a letter to us in which he summarised his feelings about three years of fortnightly, obligatory teacher-training sessions:

'It was like being invited to the Director of Studies' party: you brought a bottle of wine and sometimes you got to open it.'

In other words, in teacher training as opposed to teacher development, the group leader is in control of what does and does not happen.

B Where in the humanistic tradition?

This book belongs in the frame offered by Carl Rogers to teachers of any subject. In his last book before his death, *Freedom to Learn for the 80's*, Rogers defines its purpose thus:

' – it aims towards a climate of trust in the classroom in which curiosity and the natural desire to learn can be nourished and enhanced.

– it aims towards a participatory mode of decision-making in all aspects of learning in which student, teacher and administrator each have a part.

– it aims towards helping students to prize themselves, to build their confidence and self-esteem.

– it aims towards uncovering the excitement in intellectual and emotional discovery which leads students to become life-long learners.'

Rogerian thought has had wide influence across the professions. We feel in tune with community architects who believe that they should design for people's expressed needs, and with sports trainers who know that an athlete's physical performance is a subset of his/her mental and emotional state. These workers see their clients with their bundles of needs and wishes as the centre of the professional process, as the protagonists in the action. They do not see their clients as the *objects* of their skills. So humanistic divorce lawyers will do what they can to get the parties to conciliate rather than litigate, despite the good money that litigation brings the professional. In conciliation the couple themselves are the protagonists while in litigation the leading role falls to the lawyer.

With these principles in mind, we have come up with a hundred exercises to help students map their *own* procedures and experiences. We feel that this book, which draws heavily on feeder fields such as counselling and humanistic psychology, firmly places the learners themselves centre-stage, proposing a side-line role for the teacher. We doubt this book would have happened without the influence of Carl

Rogers, the counselling movement, especially co-counselling, the work of Earl Stevick, Caleb Gattegno, and Bernard and Marie Dufeu.

C Benefits

Let's start with the book's strangenesses. As you flick through you may wonder if you are holding a serious EFL book or some uneasy amalgam of philosophy, pop psychology and odd nonsense. Why should students spend valuable class time analysing how exactly they each eat a pizza (p.21)? What has this quaint information to do with learning English?

Benefit 1

Students say things in L2 they have never before said in L1.

Most students have never stooped/stopped to notice how they eat a pizza, how they cope with transitions from one state or event to another (p.27), how they experience the time and psychological distance necessary to correct a piece of English writing they have recently done (p.39). We invite them to think in new areas like these and then to express their thoughts and discoveries in English.

Here you have a major language learning benefit as they are unlikely to have ever expressed these thoughts in any language before. This copes with one of the major problems of the FL classroom which is the constant repetition of things already said in L1 and rehearsal for future use in L2, which often lead to both acute and chronic boredom. When small children learn their mother tongue they are constantly saying thrillingly new things.

Within the frames we offer in this book the students are saying sufficiently new things to one another and to you to stay awake inside as well as out.

Benefit 2

The English lesson is more person-centred than other lessons.

Large parts of this book involve students in exploring the most fascinating territory that exists: self. If you work in the secondary school system it is likely that only a few of your colleagues in other subjects will manage to endow their topics with personal-to-the-student relevance. So the benefit to the students and to you is that your language classes will stand out from the rest as inherently motivating and interesting. A state of attentive interest is the best garden for plants like grammar and phonology to easily and naturally grow in.

Benefit 3

These exercises reach an appropriate level of emotional depth and do not trespass beyond.

In the literature of humanistic language teaching we have books like Moskowitz's *Caring and Sharing in the Foreign Language Classroom* and Frank and Rinvolucri's *Grammar in Action Again* that sometimes make steep demands on the students in the area of self-revelation.

Some of the frames offered in this book suggest that students look at *how* they do various things. Speaking about *how* you do something can be intimate but it is a lot less threatening than sharing *what* you feel about something. This book carries forward the person-centred tradition of *Caring and Sharing in the Foreign Language Classroom* and *Grammar in Action Again*, but perhaps makes fewer emotional demands on the student.

Benefit 4

Students learn to be surprised by classmates they don't believe can surprise them any more.

In plenty of groups where students have been around together for a long time, there can be a feeling that they know each other pretty well and that old X is a typical this, and old Y is a typical that.

A clear benefit from using this book is that students really give each other surprises. Many people assume that a headache is a headache (p.18). When a person who has eye-pulsating aches realises how different a millstone-on-your-head ache is, there is genuine amazement.

Old Y is no longer just a typical that. Some of the exercises here have had the effect, in our classes, of getting students to partly emancipate from the limiting belief that 'I am human, so to be human is to be like me'.

Benefit 5

You, the teacher, prepare less, learn more and become more prepared.

The book offers you a collection of firm lesson plans to work within, and so reduces preparation time, but also offers you insights into the student unknown. You go into class with the reasonable expectation that you are going to learn something new about some of the students. Teaching language or any subject can fast get boring – teaching people never can.

Benefit 6

Many of these awareness-raising activities can be done by beginners, as the English they require is quite simple. However, some could also usefully be done in mother tongue. The use of mother tongue is justified, we feel, in terms of student self-awareness. In some situations to tell students to use mother tongue for a small part of the class time makes them feel better about using English the rest of the time. (We have a colleague, Jim Wingate, who orders his teenage classes to speak mother tongue for two minutes at various points in a 45-minute lesson – this procedure gives him control of which language they are speaking.) Here you have a teacher resource book that caters for beginners as well as higher levels. The best place to look for exercises useful to beginners is in section 2 **Language and learning processes** and in section 3 **Group process**.

D What's where?

With this book, rather than offering you new content, we are suggesting you can generate genuinely interesting text from your students by asking them to explore their own processes in and out of class.

The area has so much potential that you might want to offer process exploration as a self-contained elective course. You might want to run student process exploration as a quarter of the course alongside your current textbook. You might want to occasionally dip into the book for an exercise that is particularly relevant to certain people in your group – a good example would be *Loud and quiet* (p.84), an activity designed to help people notice where they come on a scale from shyness to over-confidence. Often realising that he or she is the loudest in the group has a calming effect on a student.

1 Everyday process

The exercises here ask students to find out for themselves about general processes and patterns in their lives. Let us offer you an exercise to show how straightforward and yet complex the exercises in this section are:

> What are the five to seven last things you do before leaving your house or flat, say in the morning? Is there an invariable order in which you do them? The order must be psychologically comfortable in some way. How functional is it?
>
> Now choose a person whom you know very well and write down the last five to seven things she or he does before leaving home.

Sometimes learners are amazed at how differently from each other they behave, and sometimes they are amazed at the sameness and differences between their last seven things and the other person's last seven things.

When learners do this type of exercise and compare their findings, they discover all sorts of interesting things about their own ideas, values and fears. The exercise above is, incidentally, a natural, free drill for the present simple.

The section includes a lesson on how to discover, analyse and imitate excellence in others (p.17), one on how people shoulder (or not) responsibility (p.22), and one on the pain-shapes headaches take (p.18).

We feel that an examination of routine process is a good way into the area but you may decide it is more relevant with EFL students to launch straight into the second section.

2 Language and learning processes

We believe that language is a way of *being* and not a form of *having*. A person who has learnt Latin academically *has* it but does not *exist in* it: for this person the language is nothing but kilos of possessed exponents linked by intellectually, consciously applied rules.

In *Teaching Myself*, pp.10 – 11, Bernard Dufeu lists the differences he sees between:

A PEDAGOGY OF HAVING and	A PEDAGOGY OF BEING
hierarchical relationship	empathetic relationship
teacher imposes, controls, demands responses	animator suggests, and responds to demand
vertical transmission of intellectual understanding	horizontal expansion of practical knowledge
teaching on a conscious level	conscious and unconscious learning
language learnt, transmitted by textbooks	language lived, approached through experience

(This is less than a third of Dufeu's complete list.)

If language is *being* then human relationship is a central governing factor. It is just this sort of area we ask the student to work on in *When do I speak well?* (p.69). In the exercise the student is asked to rate each statement given according to how far they agree with it. Here are a few:

- The number of people I am talking to affects my speaking.
- Certain native speakers really make me feel good/bad in English.
- The age of the people I am with makes it easier/harder for me to speak to them in English.
- The sex of my interlocutor(s) affects my performance in the language.

In another exercise in this section students are asked to bring to mind their *Language autobiographies* (p.48), how they speak L1, how many variations of L1 they speak, the different accents they use, etc. From here they move on to their relationship with L2, L3, etc. This information is interesting to each person as many have never put their thoughts together this way, and expressed them to their classmates and to you, the teacher.

The section also offers much more detailed looks at smaller areas, e.g. what happens in the mind during a *Cloze* exercise (p.33) and how to get *Distancing* from a piece you have written so as to be able to correct it successfully (p.39).

3 Group process

This is the longest section in the book and deals with the way people act on each other in the group. The section includes classical exercises taken from counselling like *Group collage* (p.75) and *Group sculpt* (p.83) but has plenty of new ones like *Yolks and whites* (p.106) in which students notice how particular classroom configurations impinge on them, making them feel comfortable or otherwise.

How closely have you asked students in your classes to explore the English punctuation system? In the activity *What are you writing to?* (p.104) they do exactly this, while also thinking about the way in which they see their classmates. Which of these punctuation marks would you want to be seen as and which is the punctuation mark other people may see you as:

!   .   ;   ,   "   /   -   ^   ?   :   [   ]   {   }   (   )   *

This section of the book is one you can usefully share with colleagues in other subject areas, as these exercises are not specifically to do with language learning.

If you work in teacher training or are a member of a teacher development group, you will find a great deal that is relevant to understanding how groups function in this section. We feel it is a useful addition to the ideas already around in Jill Hadfield's book *Classroom Dynamics*.

4 The coursebook

In tens of thousands of language classes round the globe, learners work their way through the coursebook. This section invites them to stand back and have a look at the curious book at the heart of this process. Is there a human being lurking shadowily behind the coursebooks? *Absent friend(s)* (p.109) invites students to guess what kind of people the coursebook authors are. Few writers whose book takes a year to work through are as purposefully faceless to their end-readers as coursebook writers, though they may be well-known to some teachers through conference appearances.

Self-accessing the coursebook (p.118) ends the third term or second semester with a cleansing act of reframing which turns the now used books into reclassified, self-study resource material.

If students are to spend many hours in the world of the coursebook, it is reasonable to let them see who makes them and how they are made.

5 Ways of learning

The aim of this part of the book is to have students do exercises that explore their overall learning strategies. We believe this is the first time that the work of Howard Gardner on multiple intelligences has been shared with language students. So far little has been heard in the EFL world of the pioneering work of Antoine de la Garanderie on the psychology of cognitive learning. *Four ways* (p.122) allows you to find out about his thinking alongside your language students / teacher trainees.

While the exercises in section 2 **Language and learning processes** help students to look at learning tactics, this section deals with learning strategies, or more all-inclusive learning patterns.

The exercises in this section force students to notice each other's brilliant diversity and realise that being human does not inevitably mean being the same as you.

6 **Correction**

'Mario, you are not a teacher, you refuse to correct me.' This was once said to one of us by an irate Austrian seventeen-year-old who clearly expresses a widely-held learner perception of teacher role and function. The exercises brought together here express no certainty about the when, how and if of correction. What they do is to consult the learners and to share our doubts with them.

We feel it is worth offering you a whole section on this area as the way this kind of feedback is given to the students is central to teacher–student relationships. So, in *To praise or not to* (p.147), we suggest you teach one lesson in which you give emotionally neutral correction and a second lesson in which you praise the student generously. The nub of the work is the students' description and analysis of their reaction to these two correction modes.

7 *Teacher to teacher*

Most of this book is addressed to your students via you; this last section is addressed directly to you, the teacher.

You can do some of the exercises on your own, some with a colleague you feel OK with, some with a group of colleagues, and some with students.

The issues dealt with are basic to being more confident in your teaching, but, though basic, they are often neglected. In *Creative listening* (p.158) careful listening to the student helps them come up with their own solution to a disciplinary problem. And if you're feeling under-confident, *Students love teachers* (p.167) offers a way of assessing what the students think about you. *Sharing a class* (p.164) is a way of looking at and improving working relationships with a colleague who you're teaching a class with.

Earlier in this introduction we have looked at the difference between a teacher development group and a teacher training group. If you're feeling on your own, have a look round and find a few colleagues. Fix a time and place to do a few of the exercises from this section. You've now got a support group.

Endpiece

A book of this sort is not a finished product though the authors and editors need to act as though it is. It is just a report on work in progress as far as we have taken it. In using these materials your students will lead you into new thought areas and these will in turn produce new exercises for use with the same or other classes.

You may find yourself flipping through the book, landing on an exercise, disagreeing with it and suddenly coming up with a new one.

You may read some of our rubrics and understand something quite different from what we intended – it may turn out better than we intended (this often happens).

You may hear an exercise from the book outlined to you by a friend – a new exercise may be born in the transmission.

You may want to adapt some of the suggested classroom procedures so that you can use them in a teacher training context.

All of the above are creative possibilities. Should any of them happen to you, jot the new idea down and publish it in a language teaching magazine. The magazines are screaming for good, new material.

You may come up with things you wish to discuss with us – if so contact us at:

Pilgrims House, Orchard Street, Canterbury, CT2 8AP, UK.
http://www.pilgrims.co.uk

1   Everyday process

1.1   Daydreaming

Benefits
Analysing how and why people daydream.

Students
Elementary to advanced; children, teenagers and adults.

Time
30 – 40 minutes.

Preparation
Put the questionnaire on an OHP transparency or make photocopies.

In class

1 Write the words TO DAYDREAM on the board and discuss with the group what the translation into their mother tongue is. There is a difference between the Japanese 'to lose thoughts' and the Italian 'to dream with eyes open'.

2 Dictate the following questionnaire to them.

> – Do I daydream frequently?
> – How often in a day do I daydream?
> – More in the morning or more later in the day?
> – Where do I do most of my daydreaming?
> – How long does my typical daydream last?
> – What starts me daydreaming?
>
> © Cambridge University Press 1998

Stop dictating and ask them to write a couple of first-person questions of their own. Then continue:

- How exactly do I return to my normal state of attention?
- Do I expect any results from daydreaming?
- Why do I daydream?
- Is there a difference, for me, between daydreaming and thinking?
- What differences do I notice?
- Are my daydreams dangerous?
- How much have I daydreamed during this dictation?

© Cambridge University Press 1998

3 Flash up your OHP transparency or hand out photocopies so they can correct their dictation.

4 Group the students in threes to answer the questions about themselves.

5 A general class discussion may usefully round this lesson off.

Possible follow-up

Ask the students to write a paragraph or poem on daydreaming.

Exemplification

Roy Boardman used the ideas in this unit with an advanced class in the British Council school in Naples and one of his students, Gabriella, wrote this poem:

BORDERLAND

Nightdreams have been clashing far above.
Spinning howling hurricanes
have been travelling fast
to this unknown morning.

Now
daydreams approach in peace.
Perhaps
they'll fall in crystals
     dripping
tipping tapping on the green
blades
like
soft
   rain.

1.2 I didn't know that a year ago

Benefits
Students become aware of how they make space for new knowledge or feelings and how the new fits or conflicts with the old. This awareness can then be applied to their own language-learning processes.

Students
Elementary to advanced; children, teenagers and adults.

Time
20 – 30 minutes.

Preparation
Prepare to tell your students about something (factual, conceptual, emotional) that you did not know exactly one year ago and that you do know now.

In class

1 Ask the students to stand or sit in order of their ages.
Ask them the date today.
Ask if anyone remembers what day of the week it was on this date a year ago.

2 Tell the students something you did not know this time last year but know now.

3 Ask the students to reflect quietly and think of something they had not experienced, did not feel or did not know one year ago today. It can be something very important or something very small.

4 They now turn to their 'age neighbour' and describe what it was they learnt, experienced or felt.

5 Ask the students to pair off, the eldest with the youngest, the second eldest with the second youngest and so on. Ask each person to tell their new partner about another thing they have learnt or experienced for the first time during this last year.

Variation

Ask students to think back to today's date last month. Ask them to think of something about English that they did not know then that they do now. Discussion follows.

Acknowledgement

We learnt this exercise from Jim Brims, author of *Camden Level Crossing*, who in turn learnt it from a colleague at the Bell School, Cambridge.

1.3 Excellence in others

Benefits
Evaluation of excellence in others leads to an examination – and recognition – of excellence in self.

Students
Intermediate to advanced; teenagers and adults.

Time
50 – 60 minutes.

Preparation
None.

In class

1 Tell the students about a person you know who really excels at something, either in the area of sport, the arts, thinking, dealing with people, dreaming dreams, decision-making, etc. Describe in detail an outstanding instance of this person's performance in the area designated. Explain how they achieve what they do in as much detail as possible.

2 Ask each student to think of a person they know well personally (could be themselves) who excels in some area. Ask them to define exactly what the person does brilliantly and then to describe exactly how they manage it. The more detail they can come up with the better. Interview a couple of students about the person of their choice in front of the whole class.

3 Split the class up into groups of 4 – 6 to continue describing brilliant ways of doing.

Follow-up

1 Ask each student to choose some area of excellence of their own. Stress that this does not need to be an area of conventional high value. Ask each of them to reflect and bring to mind a clearly-remembered instance of this excellence. Ask them to visualise

their performance, to hear the sounds connected with it and to re-experience their feelings at the time.

2 Pair the students and ask them to describe their own outstanding moments as fully as possible to their partner.

3 Ask the students to write up their description, either in class or for homework.

Variation

1 Get three or four outstanding learners (not necessarily language learners) to come to your class. Ask them to reflect and bring to mind the learning areas in which they most excel.

2 Question them in front of the whole group to get an anatomy of how they achieve what they do. They may be using instinctive techniques that some people in your class can pick up on and use in their own learning.

Acknowledgement

The idea of modelling on someone else's excellence is central to Neuro-Linguistic Programming. It was in this context that we learnt it.

1.4 Headache

Benefits
Discovering the diversity covered by even the simple term *headache*: we often do not realise how unique our own sensations are. We assume: 'I am human – you are human – therefore we are the same' and are surprised when this is shown to be untrue.

Students
Elementary to advanced; children, teenagers and adults.

Time
10 – 20 minutes.

Preparation
Using or adapting the 'Headache Questionnaire' below, make a wall-chart or photocopies for use in class.

In class

1 Ask people all the words and phrases they can find in their language(s) to express the idea *headache*.

2 Tell them you know what you mean by the word *headache*, but you don't know what they mean. Ask one or two students some of the questions in this questionnaire:

– Do you get headaches?
– How often do you get them?
– What time of day do you get them?
– How long do they last for?
– When did you last have one?
– Where in your head did you get the pain?
– What kind of pain is it?
– How do you know the headache has gone?
– Are people sympathetic when you say you have a headache?
– Which of these words would you use to describe a headache?

| violent | beating | slow | green | sharp | loud |
| fuzzy | shrill | jagged | dull | heavy | dark |

– Do other people in your family suffer from headaches?

© Cambridge University Press 1998

---

3 Put up the wall-chart or give out copies of the questionnaire and ask the students to use it in pairs on each other. Students are amazed at the range of pain lumped under the word *headache*.

4 Do a round-up of the vocabulary needed to describe headaches.

1.5 Lifeline

Benefits
Getting to know each other; fluency and listening practice.

Students
Intermediate to advanced; teenagers and adults.

Time
30 minutes – 2 hours.

Preparation
None.

In class

1 Ask people to draw a graph showing the ups and downs of their lives. This can be either a representation of their life in general or of

a particular aspect of it, such as career, language learning experience, life in this country or class, etc. The graph might look something like this:

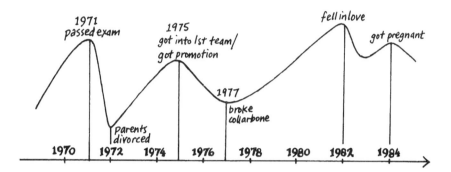

2 In groups of four, participants take the following roles:

One explains his/her graph *or the parts of it he/she chooses to talk about*;

One listens and reflects back what they have heard;

The other two give feedback on how accurate they felt the second version was.

3 They then swap roles and repeat the process.

Variation

Divide the class into groups of 4 – 6, or work with the whole group if it is small enough (up to 15). Students take turns to talk the group through their lifeline, while others ask questions or add comments from their own experience.

Possible follow-up

Students swap graphs within their groups and label each other's graphs with key points they have understood and remembered.

1.6 Pizzas

Benefits
People rarely appreciate the creativity that goes into daily living. To bring this into active awareness makes life – and other people – more interesting.

Students
Elementary to very advanced; children, teenagers and adults.

Language
The usefulness of this exercise lies in the fact that most people have never spoken about this area of experience in their mother tongue. By saying things for the first time through the medium of English, students begin to change their relationship with the language.

Time
15 – 20 minutes.

Preparation
None.

In class

1 Ask each student to draw a large pizza (or hamburger or fast food common in their country).

2 Question a student in front of the group on the exact process of eating a pizza. Students are at first surprised at a detailed focus on such a simple thing. Here are some of the questions you might ask:

– Do you eat it with your hands or with a knife and fork?
– Where do you cut into it first?
– What size and shape of chunk do you cut out?
– How do you proceed with cutting or tearing into the pizza? Do you go straight into the heart of it? Do you work round the edge? Do you go clockwise or anticlockwise?
– Do you always use the same strategy for eating pizzas or do you have more than one?

3 Tell the class your own strategy for eating a pizza.

4 Ask them to get up and mill round the room. Their task is to find two or three other people with similar pizza-eating strategies to theirs.

5 The groups report on their particular, common strategy.

Variations

1 Ask students to describe their sequence of eating and drinking during a main meal, then at home to observe a member of their family and report back.

2 Ask the students to list in writing the last seven actions they do just before leaving their house in the morning. Then ask them to compare.

3 Ask the students to list in sequence the first things they do if they get home to find the house empty.

1.7 Responsibility

Benefits
The students explore definitions of and attitudes towards responsibility.

Students
Intermediate to advanced; children, teenagers and adults.

Time
40 – 50 minutes.

Preparation
Make copies of Questionnaires A and B (see below). (You may, of course, adapt these questionnaires by omitting or changing any of the questions.)

Think of a story from your own life about responsibility, which you would be prepared to tell the group.

In class

1 Tell your story to the class. As an example, let me tell you one from my own experience:

> Claire was to spend a term staying with us. She and my daughter were both 15. We took them to Wales and I dropped them off near a waterfall. I had not realised all the rocks round it would be ice-covered. Three hours later the two girls and my son came back to the cottage, ashen-faced. Claire had slipped on the rocks and my children had just managed to hold her back from going over a cliff. I felt shock and immense relief. I had been blindly irresponsible, but nothing had happened. There was no need to phone Claire's parents in the USA.

2 Put the students in threes. Give Questionnaire A to one student in each group and Questionnaire B to another. The third student, C, is to listen and summarise what he/she has heard at the end of the mutual interview, without taking notes.

3 Ask the As and the Bs to interview each other. They work through the questionnaires asking each other questions.

4 The Cs now feedback the most important things they have heard and then go on to speak freely about their attitude to responsibility. (They have been kept dammed up during the interview.)

5 Group the students in sixes to tell stories about responsibility.

QUESTIONNAIRE A

1 When can you remember first being held responsible for something you had done? Please tell me about it.

2 If you think back over the past two years is there something for which others hold you answerable but for which you disclaim responsibility?

3 Where would you put yourself on a scale from total irresponsibility to 'I carry the whole world on my shoulders'?

4 Why do you put yourself at that point on the line?

5 When you are with foreigners, do you feel it right for them to see you as responsible for your country's actions? Do you see them as responsible for their country's actions?

6 Who would you say takes most responsibility in your family?

QUESTIONNAIRE B

1 Can you remember being blamed for something you had not done? What exactly happened?

2 Is there anybody you currently feel responsible for?

3 Do you feel different levels of responsibility as a pedestrian, a cyclist, and a car driver?

4 In what way different?

5 Think of the different bosses you have had in a work situation or teachers in a school situation. In what ways did they (not) deserve their position of responsibility?

6 When you talk silently to yourself in your head what things might the very responsible part of you say to the other parts?

© Cambridge University Press 1998

1.8 **These stressful things**

Benefits
Increased awareness of the causes of stress; sharing strategies for dealing with it; fluency practice.

Students
Intermediate to advanced; children, teenagers and adults.

Time
45 – 60 minutes.

Preparation
None.

In class

1 Have a quick, general discussion about things which cause stress. These can range from trivial things, e.g. too much homework, clothes running in the washing machine, to big ones, e.g. parents arguing, exams, redundancy.

2 Tell students individually to write down five things which cause them stress.

3 Tell them to rank their five things in order of importance.

4 Put the students into pairs and ask them to compare and discuss their lists.

5 Get them – individually again – to write another list, this time of things which cause them stress in class.

6 Tell them to rank them again in order of importance.

7 Ask them to form new pairs to compare their lists, then to choose any of the things on either of their lists and discuss ways of dealing with them.

1.9 The tempo of time

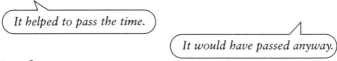

Benefits
Increased perception of time dragging or flying; recognition that this may be different for different people.

Students
Beginners to advanced; children, teenagers and adults.

Time
10 – 30 minutes.

Preparation
Take with you into class about 100 (depending on numbers) small coins (or flat buttons, or counters), or ask students in advance to bring in their own (8 – 10 each).

In class

1 Introduce the idea of time flying or time dragging. Bring in or elicit the time metaphors in the students' language(s): e.g. in Greek you say: 'My time isn't passing' to express boredom.

2 Give students an example of a coin-timeline, by putting a line of coins on the OHP or a central table to illustrate how a given time has passed for you. Explain this to them.

3 Ask the students to focus on a particular timespan, e.g. the lesson so far, or this term so far, and to express their feelings about how long or how short this time has been by making a timeline with coins. So, for example, one student made this coin-timeline to show that the first part of the lesson had gone fast for her but that the second half had really been slow in passing:

Make clear that their timelines can be straight, or circular or wavy or whatever they wish. (Coins offer flexibility and the chance to rethink: they are less permanent, and therefore less threatening, than marks on paper.)

4 In threes or fours ask the students to comment on their timelines to each other.

Variations

1 If you have a small group, ask each person to make a timeline using the other students instead of coins, spaced physically across the room.

2 Pair the students and ask them to pace out their time experience of a given period and to explain it to their partner – one person in the pair paces and the other listens carefully to the pacer's explanations. Explain, if necessary, that they can use the speed they walk, the size of their steps, and/or the direction they walk to show their feeling about the passage of time.

3 Ask the students to express their appreciation of the way time has passed as a drummed beat or a tune (they could do this one at a time or quietly, to each other, in pairs).
(The first variation works with both body and eye. The second appeals to very kinaesthetic people. Best, perhaps, would be to offer a choice of ways.)

Acknowledgement

The idea of pacing a timeline comes from John Wenger.

1.10 Transitions

Benefits
Students gain an insight into processes by viewing them from different standpoints in time.

Students
Elementary to advanced; children, teenagers and adults.

Time
20 – 30 minutes.

Preparation
None.

In class

1 Ask the group a few general questions about how they cope with the home to work or home to school/university transition. Do

people in the group 'bring the office home'? At which point on the journey home do they mentally switch from being-at-work or being-at-school to being-at-home?

2 Group the students in fours to answer and discuss these questions:
   a) How do you decide whether or not you will involve yourself in a future situation like a party, a course or a wedding?
   b) Choose an event e.g. a course or meeting, a sporting event, a long journey, the first day back at school or work, and answer the following questions about it:

- How do you feel when you are on the way to the new situation?
- How do you feel about beginnings? Think, for example, of the first five minutes of your chosen event.
- What specific things do you do to make yourself more comfortable during such a beginning? How do you manage your feelings? Please give three examples.
- How do you feel when things are halfway through, when you are midway between start and finish?
- What are your thoughts shortly before the end of something, when you know the experience will soon be over?
- And endings – how do you cope with them? Or is the word wrong for you, are endings beginnings?
- What happens in your head over the period following an experience?

Acknowledgement

I became aware of the importance of transition times in a workshop led by Michael Eales during the 1993 SEAL conference.

1.11 Weariness

Benefits

Making students aware of the many varieties of tiredness. In a tired group, addressing the question directly in this way often helps their own tiredness evaporate.

Students

Elementary to advanced; children, teenagers and adults.

Time

20 – 30 minutes.

Preparation

None.

In class

1 Brainstorm words related to tiredness e.g. tired, weary, exhausted, drained, fatigued, wiped out, etc.

2 Dictate these sentences to the group. Read each sentence twice. Ask them to write the sentences that are true for them in large handwriting and the rest in small script.

> Sometimes my body feels tired all over.
> Being bored can be very tiring.
> If I read a lot my eyes get tired.
> Speaking English too long gives me language fatigue.
> I feel exhausted after I've been very angry.
> I get travel-tiredness – I feel I am never going to get there.
> Sometimes I cannot stay awake even if I really want to.

3 Ask the students to think of all the other types of tiredness they have experienced. Examples might be: after an operation, jetlag, wheel fatigue on the motorway, the tedium of being nagged at ...

4 Group the students in fours to exchange ideas about the many forms tiredness will take, and the sorts of things that can happen to them when they get tired.

1.12 Yes, I was special

Benefits
Making a child become aware of his/her special value is at the heart of one model of teaching. By talking about this area, the students become aware of the importance they and other people attach to this kind of relationship.

Students
Elementary to advanced; children, teenagers and adults.

Time
20 – 30 minutes.

Preparation
Prepare to describe a person who treated you especially well when you were a child, a person who gave you a very special sense of your own value.

In class

1 Mention that many of us remember someone who treated us in a special way in childhood. This person could have been a relative, a family friend or a stranger. Here is an example to set you remembering. (Note: you can simplify the text or use a different one with lower levels.)

> My special person when I was 5 – 6 years old was Mr Nicholson. When my parents went round to tea it was very boring. After 30 minutes of cucumber triangles and inanities, Mr Nicholson would ask me: 'Want to come to my workshop?' For 1946 he had a magnificent carpentry workshop with power tools. We worked mostly in verbal silence but in intense communion – I remember the whine of the electric saw and the pervasive smell of the sawdust. We saved each other from utter boredom.

2 Ask how many people have brought back to mind such a person. Put the students in groups of 5 or 6 with a student who remembers such a person in each group. The students tell their stories.

3 The students get up and mill round the room. They pair off with a person from a different sub-group and retell the stories they have heard or told.

Possible follow-up

Students write up one of the stories they have heard or told, either in class or for homework.

Acknowledgement

We learnt this idea in a workshop led by Peta Gray at the Cambridge Academy. The concept of attaching special value to a person is at the heart of her very successful teaching of 'marginal' (where is the centre?) and 'difficult' students.

2 Language and learning processes

2.1 Two pictures

Benefits
Students discover the differences between their self-image as a speaker of their mother tongue and their self-image as a speaker of English.

Students
Beginner to intermediate; children and adults.

Time
10 minutes in class 1; 30 minutes in class 2.

Preparation
Come with plenty of coloured pens for everybody or ask them to come with colouring materials.

In class

In the first class, ask them to spend 10 minutes drawing themselves talking to someone in their mother tongue. Suggest they use colour. Take in the drawings without comment.

In a later class, after enough time has passed for the students to have forgotten the details of their drawing:

1 Ask them to spend 10 minutes drawing themselves talking to someone in English. Again suggest they use colour.

2 Give out the drawings from the first class and ask them to stick both drawings up round the walls of the room.

3 Ask people to go round and compare the two drawings, explaining their own to each other.

Alternatively:

1 Ask the students to think about how they are different in the mother tongue and in English, and perhaps make a few notes.

2 Get them to describe their two selves to a partner.

3 Conduct whole-group feedback on general conclusions.

2.2 Cloze

Benefits
This kind of exercise makes students more aware of their own mental processes and gives them a wider range of strategies to choose from.

Students
Intermediate to advanced; teenagers and adults.

Time
30 – 40 minutes.

Preparation
Make enough copies of the questionnaire and the cloze test for each student to have one.

In class

1 Give students the cloze test and the questionnaire and get them to answer the questions as – or just after – they do the test.

2 Conduct a full class discussion on their findings.

CLOZE TEST

A cloze test consists .... a text in .... a

number of .... have .... blanked out. These

might be chosen .... random, for .... every

seventh .... , or they might .... chosen as a

.... of testing a specific .... knowledge.

Students are .... the .... with blanks and

.... to fill them .... , usually in a set

.... of time.

33

QUESTIONNAIRE

1 How do you read the text?

a) for gist first?
b) just read until the first gap?
c) read whole thing but trying to fill in gaps 'in your head'?
d) other? Please specify.

2 When you come to a gap and you think you know the answer, do you:

a) write it in straightaway?
b) 'pencil it in' but also consider other possibilities?
c) other? Please specify.

3 When you come to a gap and you think you don't know the answer, do you think about:

a) the part of speech?
b) agreement, e.g. 'She always .... the answer.' must be 3rd person singular?
c) collocation, e.g. 'black and ....' must be another colour, probably 'blue' or 'white', depending on the context?
d) the 'sound' or rhythm of the sentence?
e) other? Please specify.

4 If there is a choice between two or more words (i.e. if you think two or more answers are correct), how do you make the final choice?

a) by sound/feel/look?
b) at random?
c) other? Please specify.

5 If you feel really frustrated, how do you normally react:

a) switch off and think about something else?
b) switch off for a while, then return to the task?
c) other? Please specify.

6 If you are working with a friend or a dictionary or thesaurus, how does this affect the process?

2.3   Noticing classroom language

Benefits
Improving the functional language the learners need to accomplish classroom tasks.

Students
Beginner to advanced; children, teenagers and adults.

Time
30 – 40 minutes.

Preparation
None.

In class

1 Demonstrate the following with a student as your partner. Your partner stands just behind you and off to one side. Both of you have your backs to the class. You start a 'conversation' writing in the air without speaking. Your partner will need to speak while you're writing to clarify what he/she doesn't get, e.g. 'Go back a bit, I didn't get it', 'What comes after ...?', 'Slow down', etc.

2 Your partner replies, writing in the air. You clarify by asking questions.

3 Pair the class and ask them to have an 'air conversation'. Give them time to have a good exchange – 8 to 10 minutes.

4 Get them to brainstorm the language they use to clarify. Write everything on the board, improving and correcting where needed. In a recent lesson a student said 'To my mind that was an A.' I then wrote on the board 'I think that's an A' as a variation in register. You end up with a pool of language the students know and have used collectively which has been enriched by additions by the teacher.

5 Now repeat the exercise. This time give the students a choice of writing in the air or using their partners' backs as a blackboard (see *Grammar Games*, Rinvolucri, p.59). The new, improved pool of language is available on the blackboard and the students will use it.

6 At the end of the second conversation students often want to do further work on the blackboard pool as they come up with new language which they want checking or enriching.

Acknowledgement

We learnt this air conversation from Simon Marshall.

2.4   Are your students CNN or MTV?

Benefits
Students notice their language role models.

Students
Elementary to advanced; teenagers and adults.

Time
10 – 15 minutes in class 1, 45 minutes at home, 20 – 30 minutes in class 2.

Preparation
Check that cable (or satellite) TV is available to a good proportion of the students in the class. If not, you need to have access to cable TV and a video.

In class 1

1 Place one chair at one end of the front of the class to represent CNN (or another English-speaking channel your students are familiar with). Place a second chair at the other end of the space to represent MTV. Ask the students to think about whether they prefer the way people speak on MTV or the way people speak on CNN. If they prefer CNN language they stand near the CNN chair, if they prefer MTV they stand by that chair. If they have no particular preference or like both, they stand somewhere near the middle.

2 Ask the people in the middle to join one or other group.

3 Give the groups 5 minutes to come up with a typical announcer/ video jockey for their channel and the times and programme that the person appears on.

4 The MTV group tell the CNN group to spend 30 – 60 minutes at home watching the video jockey selected for them, making notes in as much detail as possible of the language. The other group do the same with the announcer selected for them. They are looking for those things said that would never be said on the other channel, e.g. greetings, vocabulary items, expressions, grammar.

   (If not enough have access in their homes or through a friend then you or your students can video the chosen programme from each channel and spend time in class viewing – in separate rooms if you have access to two videos, otherwise at different times.)

In class 2

1 Each group should pool their notes.

2 Ask the students to find a partner or partners from the other group and report on their findings to each other. If the CNN and MTV groups are of different sizes the students will form sub-groups of 1 to 2, 3 to 2, 3 to 1, etc.

Acknowledgement

The above exercise was inspired by Gregory and Andy, two students in a class one of us had. Gregory had learnt most of his English from the BBC World Service and Andy from MTV, and it showed.

2.5   Course evaluation

Benefits
This is a way of making evaluation/feedback forward- rather than backward-looking and focusing on possible future improvements rather than past failures.

Students
Intermediate to advanced; teenagers and adults.

Time
50 – 60 minutes.

Preparation
None.

In class

1 Brainstorm with the whole group possible headings for aspects of the course (e.g. coursebook, supplementary materials, homework) and put these up on the board.

2 Divide the students into groups of 3 or 4. Tell them that they are a Planning Committee for the next course, and that they must discuss how they would change or improve the course and make notes under the headings they have brainstormed. Each group should consider one aspect in detail or cover all aspects more generally.

3 Students form new groups to compare their conclusions.

4 Students give you feedback on their conclusions: orally, as a group discussion, or on the board, or on posters which are put up around the room.

Variation

Giving students in groups a blank timetable to fill in often helps them to focus on the task above.

2.6 Discussions *you* learn from

Benefits
The students have the experience of being listened to by a teacher (i.e. a powerful and prestigious listener) for his or her own personal, intellectual and emotional reasons; the frame induces really thoughtful, involved language.

Students
Elementary to advanced; teenagers and adults.

Time
30 – 45 minutes.

Preparation
None.

In class

1 Instead of raising a conventional discussion topic, or one currently being aired by the media, tell the students of an area of particular concern to you, which you want to explore for your own reasons. Explain to them that you really want to hear what they have to say, and take notes during their discussion.

2 In the next class give them a summary of the things you learnt from them.

Exemplification 1

I explained to the class that my parents had always wanted to divide their property equally between their two sons. I broke with my mother for seven years, some years before her death. We then started to see each other again.

When she got too old to cope on her own in her cottage my brother took her to live with him. After her death I discovered that she had given the cottage to my brother who sold it and pocketed the proceeds. She did not tell me at the time, nor did he. While accepting her right to do what she wanted with her cottage, I felt they were both wrong to keep me in the dark about the transaction. I asked the group how they would feel in my shoes.

Exemplification 2

I brought a one-page article into class and told the group it had ideas in it which intrigued me and which I had not considered before. How did it strike them?

Here are bits of the article:

> 'We all need to be able to distinguish between what is trivial on a day-to-day, if not minute-to-minute basis. Which events in our life are important and which are not? ... Discriminating between the important and the trivial is not always easy and everyone gets it wrong on occasion ... Since we are faced with such a constant flow of events, people, places, sights, sounds, smells and thoughts, we cannot consciously evaluate them all. Instead the unconscious parts of our mind do this for us ... How do we distinguish between meaningful and meaningless things?'
>
> (from 'When the Meaning Is the Message' by Paul Keddy, *New Scientist*, 23 Oct. 1993)

2.7   Distancing

Benefits
By listening to a reading of a piece of his/her own written work, the student-as-writer is helped to take a critical distance from it.

Students
Elementary to advanced; teenagers and adults (in smaller classes).

Time
5 minutes in the first two lessons, 10 – 20 minutes in the third.

Preparation
3 – 4 minutes per student reading their text onto cassette.

In class 1

Tell the students that when they do their next piece of written work, you will be happy to take it in and record it onto cassette for them. Explain that the problem for a writer is to 'take enough distance' from their work to see what needs revising at the levels of thought, expression, and language (syntax, choice of word, repetition, etc.). To hear their text read by another person will a) focus the writer on the rhythms of the writing; b) help him/her to hear her own words as interpreted (or misinterpreted) by another.

In class 2

Collect the students' writing.

At home, read each piece of writing onto a separate cassette or, with a large class, ask the students to record each other's work. Do not correct anything. Just read what is there, giving the most sensitive reading that you can. If the students are doing the reading, tell them to do the same.

In class 3

Give back the pieces of writing together with the cassettes. Ask the students to listen carefully to the reading and to correct their work in the light of what they have noticed and understood.

Variation

If your school has a native-speaker language assistant, this is an ideal use for his/her time, especially if he/she is inexperienced in teaching, and so comes fresh to the task.

Acknowledgement

We learnt this technique from Janice Probert, head of languages in the Volkshochschule, Düsseldorf. She uses it to help students take distance from texts that they have translated.

2.8   Dreamy language feedback

Benefits
The mind takes in much more language than it is conscious of, and the recall of things unknowingly learnt boosts the learner's confidence: 'Did I really learn that?'

Students
Beginners to advanced; children, teenagers and adults.

Time
20 – 30 minutes.

Preparation
Go into the lesson having allowed yourself to enter a state of calm.

In class

1 If there is enough space and a warm floor covering ask people to lie on the floor. If this is not possible, ask them to sit physically

comfortably, that is to say with back straight, head up and both feet on the floor. Ask them to shut their eyes and listen to your voice.

2 Invite them to focus on different parts of the body, one by one, and imagine each part in turn as warm and heavy.

> Start with the left hand:
>
> > *My hand is warm*
> > *My hand is very warm*
> > *My hand is warm and heavy*
>
> Use the first person: you are speaking for the group.
>
> Lead them to thinking of these parts of the body as warm and heavy: left hand, left forearm, left arm, left foot, left calf, left thigh, left buttock.
>
> Do in the same order for the right side of the body.
>
> Use a calm, low voice, but not a sleep-inducing voice.

3 When you come to the end of the relaxation phase, gently suggest that students let their minds float over the work done over the past few hours or days and bring back to awareness any words or phrases that were important for them.

4 Students may feel they want to socialise their 'review session' or they may want to just keep their thoughts to themselves. You can give them the choice of writing a diary entry or clustering together to talk.

Acknowledgement

We learnt this from Marie and Bernard Dufeu. You will find it more fully described in *Teaching Myself*, Dufeu.

2.9　**They make it easy**

Benefits
Clarifying language feelings towards other speakers of English. (Speech is an interactive business, and A's language behaviour will naturally lean heavily on B's, especially when B is a native speaker.)

Students
Beginners to advanced; teenagers and adults (especially those who are in regular contact with English-speakers, e.g. through business or during a stay in an English-speaking country).

Time
45 minutes homework + 20 – 30 minutes in class.

Preparation
None, but this exercise is only applicable to students learning in an English-speaking country.

In class 1

Ask the students, for homework, to list 5 or 6 speakers of English with whom they have contact and to list them in order of who is easiest to communicate with. Ask them, as well, to write a paragraph about each of the first 3 speakers, explaining what precisely makes the communication easy.

In class 2

Group the students in fours to discuss the characteristics of a person who is easy for them to talk to in English.

2.10　**Exam worry**

Benefits
Establishing the degree of calm or worry in the group as an exam looms; reducing anxiety by allowing students to see they are not alone in their feelings.

Students
Elementary to advanced; teenagers and adults.

Time
15 – 20 minutes.

Preparation
You will need one A3 sheet of paper for each student.

In class

1 Put the students in groups of 8 to 12, if possible seated round a table so that they can see one another and the A3 sheets.

2 Give out the A3 sheets and ask them to each draw this continuum:

CALM ———————————————————————— SCARED

3 Tell each student to put herself on the continuum where she sees herself as she thinks about the coming exam/test. She also places all the other people in her sub-group where she thinks they would place themselves.

4 The students share their self-evaluations and their guesses about other people in their groups of 8 – 12 people.

2.11 Feel–think–do

Benefits
Giving feedback to the whole group; dealing with feelings about a given topic to clarify thought and take action.

Students
Elementary to advanced; teenagers and adults.

Time
20 – 30 minutes.

Preparation
Put three chairs at the front of the class and have the students grouped near the chairs.

In class

I hate English

I think English is very important

I love English sounds

1 Establish that the chairs represent: 'I feel that ...' (negative); 'I think that ...', and 'I feel that ...' (positive). Explain that anybody can give an opinion at any time but must sit in the appropriate chair to do so.

43

2 Introduce the subject you want feedback on. (When we did this in class we chose grammar because we felt it was an issue which split that particular class; some hated it but wanted to do more of it because they thought it was useful, some loved it and felt good at it. Other topics might be homework, spelling, group work, tests, correction, etc.) Point out any constraints from the school rules that affect the area you've chosen for feedback.

3 If necessary give a few examples around your chosen subject, sitting in the appropriate chair. For grammar I started by saying:

and then :

4 Withdraw as much as possible and let the students come up, sit down and speak when they want to. Often there is a pause at the beginning before the students 'take responsibility' and realise that you, the teacher, are sitting it out. If you intervene at this stage you might delay or sabotage the process. (Giving them three minutes to jot down their thoughts might help if you have a shy class.) Take notes of what's said.

5 Let the students carry on for 10 – 15 minutes, as long as the flow is there. Try not to intervene.*

6 Give the students your summary of their feedback from your notes. Check they agree and don't want to add anything. Add your own

opinion if you want to.

7 Then negotiate with the students on what to do; more grammar homework or whatever.

8 A good follow-up is often a grammar review or a specific lesson which covers whatever area you have dealt with in the feedback, to demonstrate that you have taken note of it.

*Note that it may be necessary to intervene on occasion and there seem, in our experience, to be three criteria:

a) If a student says we/you instead of I, ask them to talk on their own behalf and not on behalf of a perceived group or sub-group

b) If the students get mixed up between feeling and thoughts. 'I love grammar and want to do more', for instance, means that the student should clearly be sitting in the feeling chair and not the thinking chair.

c) If 2 or more students start arguing or disagreeing, explain to them that the idea is for everyone to have a chance of a say and that at this stage it's more important to listen than to disagree.

Rationale

Students often have strong feelings about aspects of learning a language. Feelings can prevent you from thinking clearly. By initially expressing your feelings it's possible to clear the way for thinking. The aim of the thinking stage is to throw up as wide a variety of ideas and opinions as possible. After thinking comes doing – the end product. Expressing feelings and thoughts leads on to doing – but it's important not to try to do too much. Doing a lot of little things often adds up to a real change – trying to do a lot, quickly, often leads to failure and so to no change.

Note that this exercise can be done on any issue – planning the future of a course in relation to feelings and thoughts about the past programme is a good subject, especially if you give out a blank timetable at the end and get the students to plan the next few lessons for you.

With this type of open-to-all feedback, it's possible for everyone to see each other's feelings and thoughts including the teacher's. Taking feedback from students individually or in groups where they don't see each other's views or your overview can lead to some people feeling ignored and to conflict. If, from written feedback, you find half the class want more grammar and half want less, then you might feel you've got it right and not change, but if the halves don't know each other's views they could all feel ignored by the teacher.

2.12 Good learning, bad learning

Benefits
The students gain insight into learning strategies by contrasting their own good and bad learning experiences.

Students
Elementary to advanced; children, teenagers and adults.

Time
30 – 40 minutes.

Preparation
None.

In class

1 Group the students in fours. Ask each person to bring to mind two good, positive learning experiences – one should be a recent one and the other should be from way back. They could be learning experiences in the family, in school, solitary or in a peer group. The students exchange experiences.

2 Ask the students to work individually and write down a description of a bad learning experience from early on. Post the descriptions round the walls so that students can go round and read them.

Alternatively, students may speak about their bad experiences and then write about their good ones.

You could also conduct a whole-group discussion at the end.

Acknowledgement

We have been to excellent sessions in which students describe what they see as positive and negative learning experiences given by Rosalind Young of Besançon and Peta Gray of Cambridge Academy. (Peta Gray co-wrote *Letters*.)

2.13 **Graphs of learning**

Benefits
Students use graphing to begin discussion of aspects of learning from within their own cognitive frame.

Students
Elementary to advanced; children, teenagers and adults.

Time
20 – 30 minutes.

Preparation
Make sure there are enough coloured pens for all.

In class

1 At a point in the course where you feel it is time to find out how the students view their own progress, tell them you want them to think of all the things that affect their learning. Do NOT be drawn into telling them anything *you* may be curious about. The choice of aspects is theirs, as it is their learning, rather than your teaching, which is to be the focus of the activity. (The variation below considers how graphs may be used to explore a mutual or teacher-led agenda.)

2 Draw a graph on the board to illustrate the general idea. The horizontal axis represents time from the start of the course till now. The vertical axis should represent some easily understood physical variable such as temperature (in degrees) or class attendance (as a percentage).

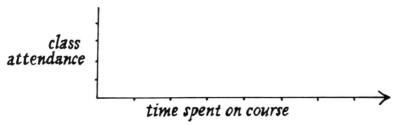

3 Explain that they are now going to produce their own graphs. Ask them to choose different coloured pens to mark in the curve of each learning variable that they have chosen. Go round and check each person understands the idea of graphing. Allow conversation where,

for example, students want to establish the precise date of some classroom event.

4 Organise groups of six to eight people and ask them to compare their graphs and to explain them.

5 Collect in the graphs to help with your thinking about the group.

Variation

We have found that though free graphing is very rich, it may be important to use the graphing exercise to put certain issues on the table. With adults we have asked them to graph aspects such as these:

- energy levels
- language tiredness
- regression to earlier age states of mind
- care about mistakes
- progress / amount being learnt

2.14 Language autobiographies

Benefits
Students' language autobiographies provide the teacher with vital indications about what has and has not worked. If you had 'M' in your class (see 1 below), it would clearly be foolish to keep correcting her. You would need to do all you could to shield her growing foreign language ego from knocks, blows and ridicule.

Students
Elementary to advanced; late teenagers and adults.

Time
60 – 75 minutes in class 1; 40 minutes in class 2.

Preparation
Go to class ready to tell your own language autobiography, the story of your relationship with language.

In class 1

1 Here, for example, is an outline language biography of a colleague at Pilgrims, to get you thinking about *your* language life-story – your class will react to *yours* much more warmly than to a stranger's:

M reckons she uses three Englishes: her Oxfordshire speech, which was a peer group language in childhood; English with an Irish accent, which she uses whenever she is with her parents, who are from Eire; and middle-class, academic English, which she uses at work and with many of her current peer group.

At secondary school M learnt French – she learnt it as a system, not a language. Her family admired her for her achievement, as did most of the people she met in France, but there was one person she met over there who gently suggested to her that she should relax more and speak more freely. M refused my switch to French during our interview – she stayed firmly in English! She reckons she has a very strong internal language monitor when she speaks French and that she suffers from what Earl Stevick calls *latho-* (mistake) *-phobic* (fear of) *aphasia* (inability to speak).

German at school was quite different for M. With French she had no choice but she actively opted to learn German. She was in a small class of 8 – 9 children. They had a native-speaking teacher who was all over the place, a real mess, but he genuinely spoke German to them.

In German she has no fear of error – when I switched to German she followed with ease and mastery. To my ear, M *is* in German, while she *has* knowledge of French.

When M went to work in Poland she spent three months in her flat studying the language intensively – she used books and TV. But then her motivation crashed because a) she realised she hated her boss and so she was unlikely to stay in Poland; and b) Polish friends and colleagues either laughed at her attempts to speak their language or corrected her to death. Neither behaviour felt OK.

2 Tell the class your language autobiography starting with your relationship to your mother tongue and its variants and then moving on to other languages you know.

3 In front of the class, interview one of your students about their language life-story. You may need to spend some time on their relationship to their mother tongue and its dialects. They may have socio-linguistic and political reasons for not being up-front about their relationship to dialects and regional languages. (The part to

do with mother tongue is usually the less conscious area of a person's language thinking but also the richest and deepest.) Spend 10 to 15 minutes on the interview.

4 Put the students in threes and ask A and B to interview C about his/her relationship with language(s). Each of the three is in turn interviewed by the other two. The interviews should not last longer than 15 minutes each.

5 For homework ask each student to write his/her own language autobiography.

In class 2

1 Group the students in fives to read each other's autobiographies – allow discussion and reaction time.

2 Ask the students to put all the texts up on the wall with a blank beside each. Invite students to go round reading and making written comments on the blank sheets.

3 Collect in the papers as they are likely to contain useful information.

Variations

1 The idea of 'restricted autobiographies' is a very generative one:
- My life story as a car driver
- Me as a cook
- Me up and down: skiing, paragliding, mountaineering, diving
- My autobiography as a person in authority
- Me and pets

2 If you are working in an English-speaking country and the students are living in host families, get them to milk limited autobiographies from their host and hostess and then report these in class.

2.15 **Language-learning experiences**

Benefits
Thinking consciously and sharing ideas about language learning, especially at the beginning of a course, makes students more aware and more able to benefit from their course.

Students
Intermediate to advanced; young adults and adults.

Time
45 – 60 minutes.

Preparation
Make enough copies of the questionnaire below for each student to have one.

In class

1 Give out the questionnaire. Check that all the students understand everything.

2 Ask students to answer the questions for themselves, in writing. Tell them they need only answer the questions they want to.

3 Ask the students to interview each other in pairs from the questionnaires, and tell them to expand on their written answers if they can.

4 Combine the pairs into groups of 4 or 6 to discuss the results of their interviews.

5 Conduct a quick whole-group feedback on the students' conclusions.

QUESTIONNAIRE: LANGUAGE-LEARNING EXPERIENCES

1 How many foreign languages have you learnt or tried to learn formally (i.e. in class)? Which ones?

2 If you have learnt only one language in this way, outline the method by which you were taught. If more than one, compare the methods. Think about a) the roles of teacher and students; b) the type and use of materials; c) the amount and type of practice; d) correction methods; e) other aspects.

3 Have you learnt any languages informally (i.e without going to classes)? If so, which one(s)? How did you do it? How successful were you?

4 Think about an effective language teacher you have had or known (this could also be a friend who taught you informally). What were the qualities that made this person a good teacher?

5 What do you think are some of the things that might make you want to learn?

6 What conclusions can you draw from the above about language learning and language teaching?

© Cambridge University Press 1998

2.16 Language-learning anxiety

Benefits
Coming to terms with fears about the language, self, the group and the teacher.

Students
Elementary to advanced; children, teenagers and adults.

Time
20 – 40 minutes.

Preparation
Make a copy of the questionnaire for each student.

In class

1 Give out the questionnaire below to the students and tell them to fill it in individually and, if they wish and have time, to write in statements of their own in the blanks left.

2 Group the students in fours to compare their ratings and their statements.

LANGUAGE ANXIETY QUESTIONNAIRE

Mark each of the statements below using this code:

Very Much Me = VMM   Rarely Me = RM
Sometimes Me = SM   Never Me = NM

1 In class

_____ In my language class I just freeze – when the teacher calls on me my mind goes blank.

_____ In tests I forget things I know perfectly.

_____ I can only speak if I'm sure it is going to be right.

_____ In the English class the only good times are when my mind is elsewhere.

_____ I'm always aware that the teacher will pounce on any mistake I make.

_____ ....

[write your own statement]

2 In general

_____ Someone speaks to me in English: I don't understand and I am scared.

_____ I can't learn English, however hard I try.

_____ People laugh at me when I do try to speak.

_____ Everybody understands more than me.

_____ I need to understand everything if I am to properly understand anything.

_____ ....

[write your own statement]

3 Studying

_____ I know I study much too hard – I can't feel relaxed about English.

_____ Learning English is really hard so I put off studying.

_____ I'm scared of failing my English course.

_____ There are so many rules I'll never speak the language.

_____ ....

[write your own statement]

© Cambridge University Press 1998

Acknowledgement

Much of the material for this questionnaire comes from 'Foreign Language Classroom Anxiety' by Horowitz, Horowitz and Cape, in Horowitz and Young, *Language Anxiety*.

2.17 What about mother tongue?

Benefits
General raising of language-awareness; exploring the different levels of skill used in the mother tongue; and the insights this can give into the use of the target language.

Students
Elementary to advanced; teenagers and adults.

Time
50 – 60 minutes.

Preparation
Select a rich, complex picture and make copies for each pair of students. The one printed below is included only as an example.

Relativity by M. C. Escher. © 1998 Cordon Art – Baarn – Holland. All rights reserved.

In class

1 Pair the students and give out one picture to each pair. If your group has many mother tongues, pair people who share a mother tongue. If some people have no partner ask them to take both L1 and L2 roles in what follows.

2 Ask the students, individually, to write half a page in their mother tongue about the picture.

3 Ask the students to swap texts with their partner and translate what the partner has written into English.

4 Tell the translators to continue the passage they have just translated, still writing in English.

5 Ask the students to swap papers and translate the second part of the passage out of English and back into mother tongue.

6 Ask each student in turn to read aloud the part of the passage in front of her that is in her L1. (Do this even if there are several mother tongues in your group.) Take careful notes on how skilful each L1 reading sounds in terms of fluency, rhythm etc.

Possible follow-up

If you teach in a secondary school, fix a time to meet the person who teaches the mother tongue to your English class. Ask them to bring specimens of the students' work in L1. Find out about your students' weaknesses and strengths in L1.

A note on allowing and not allowing the mother tongue in class:

Those teachers who ban mother tongue from their English classes may have good reasons for doing so. Perhaps translation does slow down the learning process – we have all met speakers who only relate to L2 via L1 (they speak painfully slowly and comprehend the same way).

But how we deal with the problems students face in learning English may depend in part on knowing how they perform in the equivalent areas in L1.

The lesson proposed above shows at least:

- how rich the student's vocabulary is in L1
- how she composes in L1
- how she spells in L1
- how well she reads aloud in L1
- how well she relates L1 to L2

If a Spanish-speaking student finds spelling hard in English this may be because English is intrinsically harder to spell in. However, if she is a bad speller in Spanish too (Spanish has a very logical sound-to-symbol correspondence), then maybe she is a weak visualiser. In this case she needs visualisation exercises to help her spelling forward in both languages.

If you are teaching the flute to a clarinet player then her fingering and breathing with the first instrument is of more than academic interest to you.

For those who teach multi-lingual groups, Michael Swan and Bernard Smith's *Learner English* gives a useful glimpse of the way 20 languages work syntactically, lexically and phonologically.

Acknowledgement

The translation technique above comes from John Morgan, co-author of *The Q Book*. It offers the translator almost instant authorial help and binds the translator and the author in a highly personal relationship.

2.18 Spoken three-ways

Benefits
This is a student-centred approach to improving oral competence. Giving the role of examiner to the students can help build their confidence, while the role of the observer helps them to become more critically aware of their peers', and ultimately of their own, performance.

Students
Elementary to advanced (especially those preparing for Cambridge or similar oral exams); teenagers and adults.

Time
30 – 50 minutes.

Preparation
If students do not have an exam preparation textbook containing the kinds of photos used in the oral test (for Cambridge First Certificate and Cambridge Advanced English), find enough suitable photos or magazine pictures for each student to have one or two.

In class

1 Have a general class discussion about how to describe a photograph well in an oral test, and the kinds of things an examiner is looking

for, i.e. oral fluency (possibly broken down into sub-skills), general confidence, eye contact and body language, grammatical accuracy, phonological accuracy, etc. You or a student should act as class secretary to write these up on the board.

2 Divide the class into groups of three. Give each student one photograph and tell them to write a few questions about it, without showing their photos to each other.

3 Students take it in turns to assume the role of examiner, examinee and observer. The examiners show the examinees their photo, give them a minute or two to think about it and then ask them their prepared questions. Observers watch and take notes on how examinees could improve their performance, referring particularly to the items on the board. After each turn the observer gives the examinee feedback based on their notes. They can also give feedback to the examiner.

4 If there is time, repeat the whole process using a new set of photographs or magazine pictures.

Monitor throughout all stages, first checking and correcting the written questions where necessary, then making a note of general areas which require work or practice. Conduct a short discussion on these at the end of the session.

2.19 Your own ABC

Benefits
The realisation that English is all around, even in the home environment, and of how much students can discover for themselves.

Students
Beginners; young children, teenagers and adults.

Time
30 minutes, from time to time.

Preparation
Ask each student as homework to have a look round their house, on TV and in the streets and copy down one English word or phrase. It's important to make clear that the word should be English rather than another foreign language or a brand name. Ask them to find out the meaning of the word by asking someone or looking in a dictionary.

In class

1 Get the students in turn to shout out the spelling of their words or phrases to you, and write them up on the board. Ask them where

they saw the word and write the place next to the word (e.g. TV, T-shirt, street).

2 Teach the pronunciation of the words and ask the students to explain the meanings. If they can't manage, help them or let them translate.

3 Get them to group the words/phrases alphabetically by initial letter e.g. A – F, G – L, M – R, S – Z, and write them in their notebooks on a separate page for each group.

4 Hand out sheets of A3, one for each alphabetical group, and ask small groups of students to be responsible for one group of words/phrases each. Ask them to copy their words on to the sheet, so that they are clear and visible but so that they leave space for other words.

5 Put the posters up round the room.

6 Repeat the exercise from time to time, getting students to add to the lists in their notebooks and on the sheets on the wall. Also 'test' them from time to time on the words.

Note that the number of alphabetical groupings/sheets of A3 will depend on the number of students and the amount of space you have.

2.20 Playing with meanings

Benefits
By playing with the meanings and potential meanings in a sentence about themselves, the students discover a great deal about both themselves and the language.

Students
Elementary to advanced; children, teenagers and adults.

Time
15 – 30 minutes.

Preparation
Have ready a long sentence that captures something that the group, or a member of the group, is feeling at this point in the course.

In class

1 This was a long sentence we used on Day 2 of an intensive course in the UK:

I HAVE BEEN HERE FOR A DAY AND A BIT, IN FACT SINCE SUNDAY THE 20TH AUGUST, AND I HAVEN'T YET HAD REALLY ENOUGH TIME TO GET USED, AGAIN, TO THE ODD, BIZARRE, DIFFERENT SOUNDS OF ENGLISH, SOUNDS THAT ARE SO DIFFERENT FROM THE MELLIFLUOUS MUSIC OF MY MOTHER TONGUE.

2 Put the sentence you have prepared up on the board. Ask a couple of people to read it aloud. Answer any comprehension questions.

3 Tell the students they are going to reduce the sentence down to perhaps one word, using the following strict procedure:

- any student may propose the deletion of one word or of two or three *consecutive* words
- the teacher rubs the word(s) out immediately (without considering the correctness or otherwise of the remaining sentence)
- the student who proposed the deletion reads the remaining text *aloud* to check that it is a) grammatically correct; and b) still meaningful (though the meaning WILL change).

At this point one of several things may happen:

- the deletion leaves a correct sentence, in which case the teacher silently waits for another student to propose another deletion
- the reduced sentence as it stands is not acceptable to the student who proposed the deletion, and/or to the rest of the group. In this case the teacher allows any discussion that arises, then restores the deleted item(s) and waits for another proposal
- the reduced sentence is incorrect, but accepted by all the students. Here, the teacher simply puts back the words taken out, leaving any explanation to a later time.

The process continues until the students get the sentence down to one word or until the group (and you) are satisfied that no more words can be taken out.

Acknowledgement

This exercise comes from the work of Caleb Gattegno, originator of the 'Silent Way' of language teaching. Fuller exemplifications may be found in Morgan and Rinvolucri, *Once Upon a Time*, where it is used to deconstruct a long narrative sentence, and Rinvolucri, *Grammar Games*, where the focus is on syntax and intonation (some deletions require a major change of intonation when you read the remaining sentence).

2.21 Rough copy

Benefits
The changes, crossings-out, and so on in a rough copy show part of the writer's thought process: here, the students are invited to observe, and pay respect to, their own and others' processes.

Students
Elementary to advanced; children, teenagers and adults.

Time
3 minutes in class 1; 20 – 40 minutes in class 2.

Preparation
In some cultures people work with pencil and eraser, or with word processors, which means that there is no record of changes and mental jumps. Ask such students to work in ink or biro, so that the changes they make are apparent. Apologise to them for asking them to produce messy work.

In class 1

Ask the class to do a piece of writing as homework, but NOT to make a fair copy. Tell them you want them to bring their rough copies to class.

In class 2

1 Group the students in fours. Ask them to look through each other's compositions and to answer these questions:
   • what has the person changed and why?
   • how has she changed it?
   • are all the changes improvements?
   • is the handwriting of the correction the same as or different from the handwriting of the rest of the text?

2 Bring the students together, to share what they have noticed about the crossing-out, replacing, correcting process.

Acknowledgement

The activity was inspired by a workshop Graham Palmer gave in Cambridge in summer 1994.

2.22 Spelling test

Benefits
Participants realise they are not the only ones with spelling problems. Thinking and talking about these problems can be the first step towards overcoming them.

Students
Elementary to advanced; children, teenagers and adults.

Time
20 – 30 minutes.

Preparation
Make a list of words whose spelling you know causes difficulty for at least some members of the group. These could be taken from homework or previous lessons.

In class

1 Tell students to draw up columns on a blank sheet of paper, with the following headings:

| a problem for me | a general problem | not a problem |

2 Dictate the words, telling students to put each one in the column that seems most appropriate to them, in terms of their spelling.

3 Students in pairs or small groups discuss where they have put the words and why, try to agree on the correct spelling (possibly using a dictionary), and help each other with any rules or mnemonics for future reference.

2.23 **Study habits**

Benefits
Students get to know more about their study habits.

Students
Elementary to advanced; children, teenagers and adults.

Time
40 – 50 minutes.

Preparation
Make sufficient copies of the Study Habits Questionnaire (below) for all the students.

In class

1 Give the students the questionnaire and ask them to complete it in silence.

2 Ask them to compare in threes and discuss their answers.

3 Have a general discussion with the whole group about what they have found out.

STUDY HABITS QUESTIONNAIRE

(some of these questions may seem irrelevant to you – if so, don't answer them)

1 Do you plan when you are going to study?

2 How far ahead do you plan?

3 Do you prefer to study late at night or early in the morning?

4 How do you put off starting work? If you have several techniques, list them.

5 What settings do you like studying in?

6 Do you like to be away from people or do you prefer to study with one or more friends?

7 Which types of background music do you find it impossible to study with?

8 What sort of temperature do you like to study in?

---

9 And what about light?

10 If what you're doing is hard, do you prefer to finish it anyway or do you have a set time limit at which you stop, however far you have got?

11 Do you drift off into daydreams while studying? If so are they mostly voices and sounds, or do you tend to see pictures?

12 If you are concentrating for a long period do you prefer:
   no breaks?
   several short breaks?
   one or two long breaks?
   something else?

13 What do you think about while you are taking breaks?

14 How do you bring an hour or two of studying to an end?

15 In the area of learning English, which of the following are you best at? Put a number between 1 (very bad) and 10 (excellent) against each item:
   doing grammar exercises
   learning vocabulary by chanting
   learning vocabulary by creating pictures
   talking to yourself in English
   dreaming about writing a composition
   planning a composition
   writing the middle part of the composition
   concluding the composition
   checking a composition after you have finished it
   learning a poem by heart
   listening to a text and answering questions on it
   reading a short, hard text
   reading a long text

Add your own ideas.

Acknowledgement

The questionnaire draws on several ideas proposed by Sheila Fox.

2.24 Students write their own exam papers

Benefits
Students get into the examiner's mind; they become aware of how exams work and expand their vocabulary.

Students
Lower intermediate to advanced (especially those preparing for Cambridge First Certificate or Cambridge Advanced English); teenagers and adults.

Time
50 – 60 minutes.

Preparation
Using books of test papers or copies of past examinations, blank out all the alternative answers to the multiple choice cloze questions, but leave the letters A – D and spaces. Provide enough copies for each student to have one and take these and dictionaries (and if possible, a thesaurus or two) into the class. (See sample below.)

In class

1 Using their previous knowledge and the dictionaries, students in pairs fill in possible sets of answers for 4 or 5 (depending on numbers in class) of the gaps in the cloze. Some pairs work on gaps 1 – 4, others on gaps 5 – 8, others on gaps 9 – 12, etc. (It is to be hoped that students will naturally find the right answer, which will be included as one of their alternatives, but you may need to help them here.)

2 Students take turns to dictate their words to each other, so that they all have a complete test.

3 Students do the test in the normal way, and then conduct their own feedback, either as a whole class or in two smaller groups.

Example cloze test

(from *Focus on Advanced English – New Edition* by Sue O'Connell)

Gladys, The African Vet

Last year Gladys Kalema became the Ugandan Wildlife Service's (0) ... (and only) vet after (1) ... from the Royal Veterinary College in London. She was the first person to fill the (2) ... for 30 years and, at the age of 26, easily the youngest.

If Gladys did nothing else, caring for the world's (3) ... population of 650 mountain gorillas would (4) ... justify her wages. Since the 1970s gorillas have (5) ... severely from war and poaching. Now for $150 each, tourists can be led through the forest and (6) ... within five metres of a gorilla – no closer, for (7) ... of transmitting diseases such as measles and flu.

The gorillas here make a small but viable population. (8) ... in the national parks the usual animals, elephants, rhinos, giraffes, are either not there or present in (9) ... numbers which are dangerously out of (10) ... with the creatures around them. If Uganda stays calm, wildlife may, in (11) ... , return by itself. But Gladys believes the country cannot wait. Animals must be brought in to (12) ... tourism and provide (13) ... to expand her work.

Despite her difficulties, Gladys feels more useful and fulfilled than she would be anywhere else. 'At this moment, my friends from vet school are reading the best way to (14) ... a cat or dog, and here am I planning to translocate elephants. In my small (15) ... I am part of the reconstruction and rehabilitation of my country.'

```
0  A ............  B ............  C ............  D ............

1  A ............  B ............  C ............  D ............

2  A ............  B ............  C ............  D ............

3  A ............  B ............  C ............  D ............

4  A ............  B ............  C ............  D ............
```

etc.

2.25 Time management 1

Benefits
Assessing and choosing how to spend time learning English.

Students
Lower intermediate to advanced; teenagers and adults.

Time
50 minutes.

Preparation
Each student needs 4 different coloured markers and a large piece of paper or card.

In class

1 Explain that the four different coloured markers represent four types of contact with English:
   – the school
   – self-study
   – personal interest
   – the environment

The four will need defining by a brief discussion with the class since they are not mutually exclusive and there can be overlap. Broadly we suggest the following categories for the purpose of this exercise:

> The school
>
> All class time and all homework and self-study periods that are part of the school timetable.
>
> Self-study
>
> All formal study that students do off their own bat: working from grammar and other reference or self-study books, listening to CNN and noting down vocabulary and so on.
>
> Personal interest
>
> Anything done for pleasure through the medium of English. Reading a novel or a newspaper, listening to music with English lyrics, watching English-language movies and so on.
>
> The environment
>
> Any English that the students come across: faxes and telephone calls in their job, being asked the way by tourists in the street, labels on products, advertisements and so on.

2 Ask the students to take the last seven days and mark them backwards across the top of their paper and to mark their waking hours down the left-hand side. So if the day you're working on is a Wednesday, their paper should look like this:

	Tuesday	Monday	Sunday	Saturday	Friday	Thursday	Wednesday
Midnight							
6pm							
12 noon							
7.30am							

Check with individual students: if the previous week has not been typical because it included a holiday or period of illness or heavy family commitment, ask them to go back and choose the most recent typical working week.

3 Ask the students to work individually. Working backwards through the week they should colour code when they spent time on English in various ways. Each colour represents one of the above four categories: the school, self-study, personal interest and the environment.

4 As people finish, get them mingling and explaining their grids and discussing how happy they are with how they spend their time in English.

Rationale

Most people feel pressured and uncertain about their progress at least some of the time they are learning English. Having a look and getting an overview of how you spend your time often makes you aware of how happy you are and accept that it is largely your choice as to how you spend it. Raised awareness of how the time is spent and how much choice there is does, of course, provide the first step to change, if the individual chooses to change.

Note that if your course is extensive you can look at a month rather than a week.

2.26 **Weak points, strong points**

Benefits
The students reflect on their strengths and weaknesses as language learners and share these with their teacher.

Students
Elementary to advanced; children, teenagers and adults.

Time
30 minutes homework three or four times in a course.

Preparation
None.

Early in the course, ask your students to write letters to you about what they think they are good at as language learners and what they think their weak points are. Explain that only you will see these letters. Take the letters in and keep them.

Repeat the exercise two or three more times at intervals through the course. The last time you do it, give all their letters back to the individual students.

Variations and follow-ups

Keeping the letters until the end of the course before returning them has the very positive effect of giving the students a clear record of how they have changed – as learners and as language users – over that period. At this point, write each student a reply, commenting on what they have written and sharing your own experiences of learning. You may feel, however, that it is more appropriate to reply to their letters as soon as you receive them. In this case, in a large group, it would perhaps be better to invite letters from just 5 – 6 students every few days.

Acknowledgement

We learnt this very open frame from Anna Maria Cirillo, a teacher trainer in Naples.

2.27 **When do I speak well?**

Benefits
Students explore the optimum external and internal conditions for
listening and speaking. The lesson assumes they have had contact with
people who normally speak English – if this is not the case, the lesson
is not for them.

Students
Elementary to advanced; teenagers and adults.

Time
40 – 50 minutes.

Preparation
Make copies for each student of the Speaker Feeling Profile (see
below).

In class

1 Give the students the Speaker Feeling Profile below and ask them to
work through it individually, adding factors that occur to them as
being important in their case.

2 Ask them to work in groups of 3 or 4 and compare a) their findings
about the statements below; b) the new statements they have
written.

Speaker Feeling Profile

Cross out the statements you find irrelevant and <u>underline</u> any you find highly relevant. Please write in statements of your own in the gaps.

Physical and emotional
The weather affects my speaking and listening in English.
How much I have slept affects my performance in the language.
Change of mood makes me speak and listen differently.
Headaches, stomach aches etc. adversely affect my way of listening and speaking.

....
[add your own statement]

Other people
Feelings about the behaviour of native speakers of English affect my speaking and listening.
The number of people I am talking to affects my speaking.
Certain speakers really make me feel good/bad in English.
The age of the people I am with makes it easier/harder for me to speak to them in English.
The sex of my interlocutor(s) affects my performance in the language.
The attitude of the speaker(s) to the way I use English affects my fluency.

....
[add your own statement]

Setting and topic
Knowing that the other person or people speak(s) my language well affects the way I use English with them.
What we are talking about affects my ability to speak and listen in English.
How well I know the other speaker(s) affects my speaking.
The place we are in affects my use of English.
The amount of time I feel I have to express myself makes a lot of difference to me.

....
[add your own statement]

I have language good days and language off-days.

....
[add your own statement]

© Cambridge University Press 1998

3   Group process

3.1   Anonymous envelopes

Benefits
Quick, simple way of giving and getting feedback which doesn't rely on language.

Students
Beginners to advanced; children, teenagers and adults.

Time
10 minutes.

Preparation
Take a pile of envelopes to class.

In class

1 Draw boxes on the whiteboard with a face in each one like this:

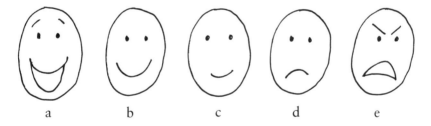

a   b   c   d   e

(a = liked a lot   b = liked   c = found this OK   d = didn't like e = hated)

2 Give the students plenty of blank boxes (small pieces of paper) each, or tell them to make their own using paper, pen, and scissors or tearing.

3 Make a list of classroom activities, over, say, the last 10 or 20 hours, which you want feedback on or brainstorm them on to the board, especially if you feel students may not remember clearly.

4 Write the name of one of the activities on each of the envelopes.

5 Pass round the envelopes and ask students to secretly draw a face to represent their feelings about each activity, and put it in the appropriate envelope before passing it on.

6 When the students have finished, give out the envelopes again and ask them to count the number of different types of faces in each envelope. They then tell you the results, which you put on the board, like this:

	a	b	c	d	e	
• reading about 'Fear'	5	3	4	4	0	
• discussion: the Lottery	6	4	0	6	0	
• stress & intonation practice in lab	3	6	0	4	3	
• proverbs crossword	10	4	2	0	0	etc.

Rationale

This is a way of obtaining clear feedback on classroom activities, while maintaining student anonymity and 'isolation'. By giving feedback on their own and not seeing any results until the end, they cannot be influenced by what others have done. It is especially useful if you are not used to asking for feedback or the students are not used to giving it.

3.2 Balloon debate

Benefits
This activity makes students more aware of the component parts of their course and their own preferences about how time is allocated.

Students
Intermediate to advanced; teenagers and adults.

Time
40 – 60 minutes.

Preparation
None.

In class

1 Tell the students to draw up a list of the component parts of the course as they have experienced it and put it on the board. The list will probably include such items as grammar, vocabulary, listening. (See below for a more comprehensive list.)

2 Explain that the class is going to take part in a 'balloon debate', i.e.

they are all in a hot-air balloon which is in danger of plummeting to the ground because there are too many people in it. Each person must argue their case for staying in the balloon on the grounds of their importance to humanity. This is usually done with famous people or worthy professions, but in this case each student will represent a component of the course (see the list below) and will argue their case for staying in the course. This will then be put to the vote.

3 Divide the class into an appropriate number of groups, depending on class size and the number of items on the list (you may possibly have a chairperson in each group if this makes sense in terms of numbers). Tell them to conduct the debate in their groups while you monitor. You can stop the debate when a set number have been thrown out of each balloon, or when there is only one student left in each, depending on how well students respond.

4 Conduct whole-group feedback, in which the students discuss variations in their results, and their reactions.

List of possible components of a course:

grammar	listening	games
vocabulary	speaking	songs
pronunciation	reading	dictation
functions	writing	video
		using computers

3.3   Circle of light

Benefits
Saying goodbye to a group.

Students
Elementary to advanced; teenagers and adults.

Time
10 – 15 minutes.

Preparation
Rehearse the guided fantasy below at home, or prepare your own.

In class

1 Ask the students to sit comfortably, preferably in a circle, and to shut their eyes.

2 Lead them in this guided fantasy trip. Leave good pauses after each sentence:

> Without opening your eyes imagine the circle you are sitting in – see the people to your right, to your left and the people sitting opposite you. Feel their presence and listen to the sounds coming from them. Keep your eyes shut.
>
> Bring to mind one or two people in this group who you have not got on so well with – inside your head say whatever you want to them. Now think of the person in this group who has been most insignificant for you and say something mentally to them too.
>
> If there are things you want to say to me or the other tutors in your head, say these things too.
>
> And now imagine a circle of light is darting round the group, round the circle, touching you and each other person. Notice how warm it feels – notice where it touches you – bathe in its warmth as it flashes round the circle.
>
> And now the light is moving out through the whole of this place, along the corridors and up and down the stairs. The light from our circle is flooding through the building and now out across the city and countryside around. Let the light reach out right across the whole of this country and then out across its borders. Let the light dart and flash right around the globe moving to all the places where you know people, linking you to them.
>
> And now bring the light back into this place, this building, and back into this room. Let the light once again move around the circle from one to another. Now look, the light is settling in the centre of the circle. Watch it there in the centre of our circle as it gently loses brightness and dies down. Now it is just a pin-prick ... The work we have been doing together is over.

Acknowledgement

We learnt this closure technique from Hazel Guest at a Trans-personal Psychology workshop in Cambridge in January 1993. It particularly appeals to people who do a lot of inner dialogue in their heads though people with visual preferences and kinaesthetic people are also well catered for.

3.4 Group collage

Benefits
Students create something of their own in a relaxing 'nursery school' atmosphere, which acts as a springboard for them to be able to talk about themselves.

Students
Beginners to advanced; children, teenagers and adults.

Time
45 minutes to two hours (see note below).

Preparation
Collect a pile of magazines, one large sheet of cardboard per student, pairs of scissors, Pritt Stick or glue, and Tipp-Ex, or ask the students to come prepared to the lesson with them.

In class

1 Tell the students that they are going to make a collage, by cutting up pictures and words and sticking them on to the cardboard. The collage should represent how they feel at the moment, or how they identify/see themselves. Each student should find a quiet space to do this, spreading out into any available extra space. Give a time limit but let the students take a break when they finish.

2 After the break, participants sit in circles and talk each other through their collages. Alternatively, this could be done as a mingle (i.e. with students walking round and talking to each other) or the collages put up on the walls.

Note

This activity can be used at the start of a course as a getting-to-know-you exercise. It is also useful at times when a group is flagging mid-course. If it seems too consuming of class time, the first part could be done outside class, as preparation.

Acknowledgement

We first learnt this exercise from Dave King and Larry Cole on a Counselling in the Development of Learning course.

3.5   Does this teacher help me?

Benefits
Through analysing 'teacher talk', students explore attitudes towards students.

Students
Elementary to advanced; teenagers and adults.

Time
30 – 40 minutes.

Preparation
Make a copy of a lesson transcript for each student.

In class

1 Ask the students to read the lesson transcript and to underline the bits that tell them most about the teacher. (Alternatively, use a similar transcript from one of your own lessons.)

2 Group the students in fours and ask them to compare what they have underlined.

3 Tell each student to re-write the text individually, changing or omitting the teacher bits they don't like and adjusting the student responses accordingly.

4 The students compare their rewrites.

LESSON TRANSCRIPT

TEACHER: What did you do, Fatima?
FATIMA: I cleaned my house.
TEACHER: You cleaned your house AGAIN? That's all you ever do, isn't it? You are always cleaning your house!
FATIMA: I cooked the dinner.
TEACHER: Did you go shopping?
FATIMA: No shopping.
TEACHER: I DIDN'T go shopping.
FATIMA: I didn't go shopping.
TEACHER: (to Student 2): What about you? At the weekend ... what did you do at the weekend?
STUDENT 2: I was visiting. I was visiting my friend.

TEACHER:	I went to visit my friend.
STUDENT 2:	I went to visit my friend.
TEACHER:	Good. (to Student 3) What about you? What did you do at the weekend?
STUDENT 3:	I went to visit my brother.
TEACHER:	Your brother? 'I went to visit my brother.' That's very good. And what did you do when you visited your brother?
STUDENT 3:	Talk ... erm ... er
TEACHER:	What?
STUDENT 3:	Um ... er I ... I eat and ... this is speak English very hard. It get better, it gets better; it gets easier. It become easier. Today difficult, tomorrow not so difficult, next week ...
TEACHER:	Oh, it's very hard, very hard, very hard, very hard. But quite easy, next year very easy. Where does your brother live?
STUDENT 3:	um ... er ... nine ...
TEACHER:	Where does he live?
STUDENT 3:	Nine, in Sheffield nine.
TEACHER:	Oh, in Sheffield nine.
STUDENT 3:	No, in Sheffield shree ... shree.
TEACHER:	In Sheffield Street?
STUDENT 4:	No, in Sheffield three.
TEACHER:	Oh, in Sheffield three!
STUDENT 3:	No, in Sheffield nine.
TEACHER:	(to Student 4) So you got it wrong!
STUDENT 4:	Yes.
TEACHER:	Yes, that's what happens when you answer for somebody else, isn't it?

© Cambridge University Press 1998

Acknowledgement

Thanks to Sheila Fox, who had this transcription made.

3.6 **Ducks and pigeons**

Benefits
Exploring the way we project on to each other by looking at the way we project human characteristics on to animals.

Students
Elementary to advanced; teenagers and adults.

Time
50 – 60 minutes (excluding any time taken to get from the classroom to the observation place).

Preparation
Choose a group of animals that you can easily take your class to observe and feed: ducks, pigeons, or grey squirrels are good options. On a sharp day in a cold winter, feeding any birds that land to be fed is another option. If you decide to work with animals like ducks that may get fed by park attendants, it may be worth checking with them that the animals have not been fed just before your observation period. You may find it interesting to check out with a zoologist colleague how the species you have chosen behaves at feeding time: pecking order, male versus female, young versus old, etc. Get bread or other suitable food to give to the animals.

In class

1 Explain to your students that you want them to pair off in preparation for 20 minutes' observing animals: their task will be to choose *one* animal per pair and together observe its behaviour while the animals are fed.

   Explain that they should take notes during the observation and that the reason for pairing them is to make sure the observation is reasonably accurate. Tell them the first thing they will need to do is to identify the distinguishing marks of their particular animal so as not to lose sight of it.

   Ask them to take notes only of what they see and hear. This is animal observation, not short-story writing.

2 Take them to the observation point. Feed the animals so the students can take notes. Come back to class, and ask them on the way to compare their observations so that each pair is ready to report an agreed body of information.

3 Ask the pairs to give their reports to the whole group. Accept simple observations but question all *interpretations* – ask for the facts to back them up. Question all observations that assume the animals observed are people: sentences like 'my duck felt ...' are very suspect.

4 Ask the students what they observed about themselves as observers. How much did they project their own feelings on to the animals observed? How much were they really observing the animals as they are?

Variations

If you cannot easily find place or time outside the classroom for observation:

1 Ask those students with pets at home to spend a little time in close observation of their pet and to report back to class. Be as strict as in step 3 above about questioning *interpretations* rather than observations of behaviour.

2 Bring in a bag of potatoes – one potato for each student. Get each student to choose a potato, study it and write a detailed description of it. Then ask students to tell a partner about their potato or get them to swap written descriptions. Collect in all the potatoes, then get students to retrieve either their own or their partner's potato.

Follow-up

Ask the students, in pairs if possible, to report on purely human events. Tell them to restrict their observations to five-minute periods. Examples might be:

- off-the-ball behaviour by players during a football match
- pedestrians walking in a crowded street (e.g. how do people avoid bumping into each other?)
- young children in a play area
- behaviour at a formal or organised event (e.g. a wedding, a political meeting, an auction)

3.7 If you were a flower

Benefits
Participants share perceptions of each other, which can help develop trust.

Students
Intermediate to advanced; children, teenagers and adults.

Time
20 – 30 minutes.

Preparation
None.

In class

1 One student chooses a category such as 'flower' and everybody writes on a slip of paper what flower they would like to be. These slips are put in an envelope, shuffled around and then read out by somebody.

2 Students then make suggestions like:
'I think ... is (would like to be) an iris because ...'
If this is correct, the person acknowledges it. These suggestions can be made round the circle or at random.

3 When everyone's identity has been established, you can move on to another category.

Variation 1

Offer students different sets of possibilities, from which they choose their identity. Students then group themselves into sets to discuss their choices, before re-grouping to form mixed-set groups and exchange ideas.
  Other categories for this activity might be:

water (river, ocean, waterfall, pond, icicle, cloud, teardrop ...)

vehicle (train, bicycle, pram, wheelbarrow, Rolls Royce, skateboard ...)

musical instrument (violin, piano, trumpet, harp, clarinet ...)

colour (green, yellow, pinkish white ...)

time (hour, minute, week, century, tea-break, week-end ...)

insects (mosquito, bee, gnat, ant, butterfly ...)

meal (banquet, snack, English breakfast, hamburger, midnight feast ...)

Variation 2

With a willing group, the metaphorical frame of this activity can be a powerful tool to bring out and discuss the students' perceptions of you as their teacher, and of teachers in general:

1 15 to 20 minutes before the end of the session, ask them to think back over the lesson and to decide which animals (or instruments, vehicles, etc.) they feel you have been like over the previous half hour, then, individually, to list them. As they work, make your own list of what you think you have been.

2 Ask them to share their perceptions of you in groups of four.

3 Ask three or four people to explain their perception to the whole class. Then tell them how you felt yourself to be at different moments in the lesson.

4 In a later session, ask the students to use the insights they gained in this activity to bring back to mind other teachers they have had, and to discuss how their view of learning and self may have been influenced by these teachers.

Acknowledgement

I learnt Variation 2 from Christine Frank, co-author of *Challenge to Think* and *Grammar in Action Again*.

3.8 Good gossip

Benefits
Publicly focusing on a classmate's good points.

Students
Elementary to advanced; teenagers and adults.

Time
30 – 50 minutes.

Preparation
None.

In class

1 Sit the students in threes. A and B are facing each other while C is sitting with her back turned to the other two.

2 Tell A and B in each threesome to gossip in a *positive* way about C. C simply listens to what they are saying, but with her back to them. Tell them they have 3 minutes gossiping time and it must all be positive.

3 Ask the threesomes to do the exercise twice more, changing roles so that each person has a chance to be the subject of discussion.

4 Bring the whole class back together again, sitting so they can all see each other, and ask each person to report one thing said about her and one thing she wishes had been said. In reporting, she reverses positive and negative polarities, so if they had said: 'She is really helpful to other students,' she will report it as: 'They said I don't care about other students.' The result of this odd procedure is that the group listens with greater attention because they have to decode the reversed polarity.

Acknowledgement

We learnt this technique from Labiosa Cassone at the 1993 SEAL conference in Warwick, UK. She first used the technique when doing a management consultancy in a company where things were being much soured by nasty gossip.

3.9 Group sculpt

Benefits
Bringing out into the open people's feelings about the group, thus helping the group to gel and develop mutual trust.

Students
Intermediate to advanced; teenagers and adults.

Time
30 – 40 minutes.

Preparation
None.

Note

Some teachers – or groups – may not wish to use this exercise if they find it either too dangerous, or too revealing, or inappropriate to their situation.

In class

1 One person is nominated, or volunteers, to be in charge of the sculpt. They give stage directions to the rest of the group.

2 The 'sculptor' tells certain individuals where they should sit or stand to represent the sculptor's perception of their position in the group. Not everyone in the group is necessarily included.

3 When the sculpt is finished, participants – both inside and outside the sculpt – ask the sculptor about the reasons behind their stage directions, and an open discussion should develop.

4 People may be moved around during this discussion, either because the sculptor decides they are in the wrong place, or through negotiation.

Variation

Group diagrams: instead of using the people themselves, participants produce a diagram of their perceptions of the group and then talk about it. The diagram can be drawn or made with slips of paper or with rods or any other objects to hand.

Acknowledgement

We first learnt about group sculpts on a Counselling in the Development of Learning course, led by Dave King and Larry Cole.

3.10 Loud and quiet

Benefits
Students and teacher consider who speaks in the group, how much and when.

Students
Lower intermediate to advanced; teenagers and adults.

Time
30 – 45 minutes.

Preparation
None.

In class

1 Clear a space and get the students to form a 'snake-like' line.

2 Write the following words on the board 'Loud Students' and 'Quiet Students'. Have a brief discussion about meaning – loud is quite negative in English when used about someone; quiet is more neutral.

3 Designate one end of the snake as 'I talk a lot in this class', the other as 'I talk very little in this class'.

4 Each student should check with their immediate neighbours – if the person is more or less talkative than they are, they should change places. If they swap they should negotiate with their new neighbour and swap again if necessary. The aim is to get to the appropriate position in the snake for them.

5 After a good few minutes, when the negotiation is mostly over, give the students another minute or so to get into position. Ask them to get to where they want to be on the line and not where they have been put by overbearing peers.

6 Initiate a short discussion on how people feel about being where they are in the snake. A good way of doing this is to ask the people at either end, how they feel and to ask the group if one end is 'better' than the other.

7 Repeat the process a couple of times to refine the discussion. This time change the definition of the ends of the snake. We've found these polarities work well: shy / not shy, 'I expect to be listened to' /

'Nobody listens to me', 'I talk more one-to-one' / 'I talk a lot in a group', 'I take the floor' / 'I never take the floor'. The loud/quiet continuum is rather crude and the additional choices give a perspective and add to the discussion.

8 Finally, have everyone go back to their positions in the original continuum. Give a minute for negotiation to see if anyone wants to change places. When you've got agreement pair the students, the 'loudest' with the 'quietest' and so on down the line.

9 Explain that one student in each pair now has to talk for two minutes and the other listens in absolute silence. Do not suggest the topics. The roles are then reversed for a further two minutes' conversation. Finally ask students which they found easier, listening or speaking.

Note

This exercise originates from a group one of us was teaching. They had thought it had formed and was performing particularly well until two comments were made in a coffee break:

RW: They're all beginning to resent me and hate me, cos I talk so much – but they never say anything and somebody has to contribute.

BH: I'm fed up with RW. She's the only one who talks and she talks all the time.

There are exercises which complement this one in Davis and Rinvolucri, *The Confidence Book*, Section 3: Listening to People.

Variation

If you feel the 'snake' is too confronting, you can offer students four possible groups e.g. very loud – loud – quiet – very quiet. Get them to walk round and talk about which group they would place each other in. Then ask them to put themselves in the group where they most see themselves. Further discussion follows.

Acknowledgement

We were introduced to this type of exercise by Stuart Oglethorpe who met it on a racial issues awareness-training course where the ends of the snake were 'most British' and 'least British'.

3.11 Mood-sharing dictation

Benefits
Examining shared feelings.

Students
Beginners to advanced; teenagers and adults.

Time
20 – 40 minutes.

Preparation
Have some coloured pens ready or ask the students to bring some.

In class

1 Explain to the students that you are going to give them a dictation. Ask them to write down everything they feel themselves in one colour and everything else in another.

2 Give them this dictation (or write your own on the same theme if you wish to make it longer or use richer language: see the alternatives suggested below). Dictate each line twice.

- I am tired, very tired.
- Now it is time to go home.
- And I am happy
- but a bit sad too.
- Will we meet again?
- Who knows when?
- Who knows where?
- Who knows how?
- Let's hope we do.

3 Ask them if there were any words they had trouble with spelling – put these up on the board.

4 Ask a number of students to read out their texts. The parts they do not identify with they read in a low voice. The parts they do identify with they read with volume and feeling. (The contrary instruction also works.)

Reading aloud in class can be excellent but needs to have a human purpose: this varied style of reading expresses a lot of emotion and comes very naturally to the more auditorily inclined students.

We have used this technique in several situations, when we believed that many people were sharing roughly the same feeling, for example:

- when many people in the group were getting stressed out as the date for a major exam approached;

- when many people in the group were getting lazy or listless and 'plateauing' in language terms.

Alternative sentences for dictation

The dictation element here is being used primarily as a way of getting the students to slow down and *feel* the content of the sentences, rather than as a practice or test of pronunciation and spelling. You can, of course, increase the length, number and difficulty of the sentences you dictate, but it would be advisable to remain well within the students' language ability. Here are some more varied examples on the theme of feelings towards the end of a course:

- I wish I could have learnt more.
- I can say some things more easily in English than in my mother language.
- Will we miss this classroom?
- How shall we remember each other?
- We have changed.
- Will we go on changing?

Acknowledgement

The idea of reading aloud in two voices was one we learnt from Mercedes Mardones, from Talca in Chile.

3.12 My name's ... and I ...

Benefits
Getting to know each other; thinking about what your name means to you.

Students
Elementary to advanced; children, teenagers and adults.

Time
10 – 15 minutes.

Preparation
None.

In class

Participants introduce themselves one by one, as and when they feel like it and may talk about their names, how they got them, etc. For example, 'My name's X, but I prefer to be called Y, because ...' or 'as a child, I used to be called Z, and I felt ...' or 'and I really don't like it, because ..., so I'd prefer to be called ...', etc.

Variation

Participants may add anything about themselves, not necessarily connected with their name.

Acknowledgement

I first participated in this activity at the beginning of an Introduction to Counselling course led by Isabella Bourne, at Metanoia, Ealing.

3.13 Negotiation

Benefits
Improving ways of negotiating with the teacher and giving her feedback.

Students
Lower intermediate to advanced; teenagers and adults.

Time
15 – 20 minutes.

Preparation
None.

In class

1 Write up the following three words on the blackboard:
Co-operative   Autonomous   Authoritative
Discuss with the students what they mean.*

2 Divide the class into two equal groups, one group to be observers, the other to act as students in the roleplay.

3 Choose a subject for negotiation, for example, whether every student should arrive on time.

4 Explain to the students that you and the 'class' are going to negotiate for 6 minutes; for the first two minutes you, the teacher, are going to negotiate in a co-operative way; for the second two you try to let the class be autonomous and during the third two you play an authoritative role. (The other half of the group are to observe.)

5 Do the roleplay.

6 Put the students in groups of four, two observers with two

participants. Give them six minutes to discuss the differences in the three ways of negotiating and their own preferences.

7 Ask the groups to give you guidance about how the types of negotiation fit in with your personality and how they prefer to be consulted.

Acknowledgement

Adrian Underhill introduced us to this exercise in a teacher-training context.

> *Co-operative*: you and the students work together to make a joint decision.
> *Autonomous*: the teacher gives the students total control and accepts whatever decision they make.
> *Authoritative*: the teacher takes control and makes the decision on behalf of the group. *Authoritarian* is the negative twin of *authoritative* when the decision is taken because the person enjoys power rather than considering it the best option for the group at the time.

3.14 Introducing a new student

Benefits
Establishing strong first contact between a new student and an established learning group. At the same time, the group is encouraged to empathise with the newcomer by reflecting on similar situations they have been in.

Students
Elementary to advanced; teenagers and adults.

Time
20 – 50 minutes, depending on class size.

Preparation
None.

In class

1 Introduce the newcomer by name and ask the class to spend 5 – 7 minutes writing questions to him/her. Ask them to go beyond very obvious first-meeting questions.

2 While the class are writing, take the newcomer aside (if possible to another room) and interview him/her yourself.

3 Go back together to the class and ask the students to form groups of four. Add the newcomer as a fifth member to one of the small

groups. Tell the students in the other groups that they are each to bring to mind an occasion when they were a newcomer, and to tell the other members of their group about it.

4 Meanwhile, the newcomer answers the questions written by the four students in his/her group. The small-group situation is less threatening than the whole class, and the newcomer can come close to the other four and have direct eye-contact. The attention paid by the 'established students' to the newcomer is also greater, and may give the newcomer a feeling of worth.

5 When the newcomer has answered all the questions in his/her group, form one large group and ask the students in the newcomer's group to introduce him/her to the others. Let the others ask any questions which have not already been answered so that this gradually becomes a whole-group activity.

Variations

Optionally, you may now:

6 Report to the group what you found out about the newcomer during your interview.

7 Ask each member of the class to introduce their neighbour to the new student by naming them and stating one interesting thing about them.

Note

The introduction technique you use will depend on the cultural setting you are working in.

3.15 Norming

Benefits
Acknowledging inherent divisions within the group and bringing some of their characteristics out into the open can defuse potential resentments and help the group to gel.

Students
Elementary to advanced; children, teenagers and adults.

Time
30 – 45 minutes.

Preparation
None.

Note

This activity is potentially upsetting for certain students and should be set up in the most light-hearted way possible.

In class

1 Ask the class to divide into two groups: categories could include male/female, young/mature, paid for by parents or employer / paid for by themselves etc., depending on the group.

2 Tell the participants to sit in two rows facing each other, and to observe one or two members of the other row for a few minutes. They should take notes, mental or written, on what they observe, relating to physical characteristics, clothing, nervous habits, etc.

3 After this, the groups form two separate circles to discuss their findings about the other group's 'norms' – i.e. what they have in common as a group – and then feed across to each other.

3.16 One thing I've learnt

Benefits
Participants have a chance to reflect on input and choose what they want to say about it.

Students
Intermediate to advanced; teenagers and adults.

Time
10 minutes.

Preparation
None.

In class

Towards the end of a session, participants sit round in a circle and comment on their experience, beginning 'One thing I've learnt from this session is ...'

There is no set order for speaking and no one is obliged to say anything if they don't want to. Participants speak as and when they feel like it.

Variation

I appreciate, I regret.

Use the same format at the end of a session, but instead of 'One thing I've learnt ...' participants begin their contributions with either 'I appreciate ...' or 'I regret ...'.

Acknowledgement

We first learnt these activities on a Counselling in the Development of Learning course run by Dave King and Larry Cole.

3.17 A penny for your thoughts

Benefits
This activity, like 'Daydreaming' (p.14), brings out the fact that people in groups think about many things that have nothing to do with the matter in hand and that this is both inevitable and enriching.

Students
Beginners to advanced; children, teenagers and adults.

Time
5 – 7 minutes here and there through the lesson and 10 minutes at the end of the lesson.

Preparation
Take a small bell to class or anything else that makes a friendly noise. Plan to leave time for a 10-minute discussion period at the end of your lesson.

In class

1 Tell the group you will ring your bell four times during the course of the lesson. When they hear the bell, the students are each to stop whatever they are doing and notice exactly what they were thinking/dreaming about when the bell sounded. They should make a brief note of their thought/feeling.

2 Give your normal lesson with four bell interruptions.

3 Group the students in sixes and ask them to share any of their 'bell thoughts' they are willing to. Either observe the whole group yourself or join one of the small groups.

3.18 Biography in pictures

Benefits
Drawing out quieter members of the group through their
life-stories. There are certain shy students who need help to take their
full place in the group.

Students
Elementary to advanced; teenagers and adults.

Time
5 – 10 minutes in class 1; 50 – 60 minutes in class 2.

Preparation
Before class 1, check with two or three of the quieter students that
they are willing to be interviewed about their lives. For class 2, bring
coloured pens and a long scroll of paper.

In class 1

1 Explain to the class that they are going to interview some of their
classmates. If there are 30 students in your class, then there could
be five interviewees and five groups of five interviewers. Explain
that each interviewer will focus on a particular period in the
interviewee's life. Ask the interviewers to decide first which years
they will ask the person about: A will ask about the interviewee's
first three years, for example, B about the years from three to six,
etc.

2 Tell the students they will carry out the interviews as homework, in
the breaks, before or after school or over the phone. Give them a
deadline.

In class 2

1 Give each group of interviewers coloured pens and a long scroll of
paper. Ask them to produce a frieze of pictures and words to
illustrate the life of their subject so far. The interviewees should be
available to help the interviewers when asked, so that what is
drawn and written is accurate.

2 Have the students put their friezes up on the walls. Everybody goes
round to look, read and comment.

A note on mother tongue

If you feel that, unsupervised, the students would do the interviewing in L1, and if you can spare class time, then you can, of course, have the interviews done in class. Against this, you might feel that the social advantages of the work outweigh the need for language practice.

Acknowledgement

We saw this technique demonstrated by Peta Gray, co-author of *Letters*. She used it to draw a very marginal member right into the heart of the group.

3.19 Sharing projections and interpretations

Benefits
Students and teacher alike become aware of the teacher's projections on and assumptions about students, and of how thoughts about the lesson and extraneous thoughts intermingle.

Students
Elementary to advanced; children, teenagers and adults.

Time
5 – 10 minutes.

Preparation
None.

In class

1 At one point where the students are working in small groups or pairs, and at a point when you feel you have a greater need to think about them than interact with them, take a segment of the board and jot down some of the thoughts you have about them, for example:

> I wonder if Luisa has a headache.
> Bruno's bored – he's foot-tapping.
> The group in the corner seem to be enjoying themselves.
> Looks as though Günther is in a pretty good mood today.

2 Carry on with your lesson as if what you have written on the board is not there. Five minutes before the end of the period, go over to what you have written and check out with the individuals if your

hunches are correct, half-right or nonsense. Rub the wrong ones out.

Note

This kind of exercise can be usefully done with a group where you and the students have good rapport with one another. Inevitably you will exercise some self-censorship.

Rationale

In this exercise the teacher allows the students to see his/her thoughts about them, at least in part. They are given entry to the teacher's own internal dialogue. There is little more compelling reading comprehension text than this. The exercise also allows the teacher to check out his/her ideas and projections and gather valuable feedback.

3.20 From proton to molecule

Benefits
Exploring and expressing feelings about being in different-sized groups.

Students
Elementary to advanced; teenagers and adults.

Time
60 – 90 minutes.

Preparation
None.

In class

1 Get the whole class up and miming the walk of someone who works in an environment where there are a lot of people – e.g. a waiter in a busy restaurant, a journalist in a crowded newsroom. Get them to walk around in role for 30 – 60 seconds, then shout 'Freeze!' Next tell them to continue walking for 30 – 60 seconds, but this time in the role of someone who works alone – a shepherd, perhaps – or in a very small, integrated team, such as an airline pilot or an ambulance driver. Continue with two or three more examples of people who work in smaller or larger groups.

2 Ask each student to work alone and make notes on the theme Working in Groups. Give them exactly five minutes for this and tell them the time limit.

3 Ask them to get up again and mill around. Once they are well mixed ask them to form groups of three. Tell them they have 10 minutes to exchange ideas on Working in Groups in their threesome. Time the 10 minutes.

4 Ask them to mill again and this time form groups of five to seven, ideally six. As far as possible the group of six should only contain one person from any given three (this will be possible if there are over 18 people in the class). Again they are to discuss the theme, but not necessarily reporting what was said in their previous three. The idea is to develop the ideas rather than repeat them. Discussion time: 10 minutes.

5 They discuss the theme in the full class. It is important that you sit out and do not chair this discussion. Allow 10 minutes for the discussion.

6 Ask the students to work alone with pen and paper for five minutes. Their task is to decide how they felt working alone, then in a three, then in a six and finally in the plenary.

7 Tell them to get back into the same threesomes as before. Give them 10 minutes to discuss their feelings about different-sized groups.

8 They get back into the same sixes as before and take 10 minutes discussing their feelings about belonging to groups of different sizes.

9 You call the whole class together and spend the last 10 minutes getting feedback on the whole exercise.

A note on the processes of the activity

Ideas around a theme flow differently depending on whether you are talking to yourself, to two other people, to five or six other people or to a relatively large group. Your listening task is also very different. The above organisation is different from a 'pyramid discussion' in that the students are not asked to report on what happened in the previous phase. Another significant difference is that the threes do not double up to form sixes. Each six is made up of students from various triads.

During stages 1 to 5 the students are working on a theme which exactly mirrors what they are themselves doing – what Tessa Woodward (*Models and Metaphors in Language Teacher Training*) calls a 'loop'. The second half of the lesson is purely reflexive in the sense that the students are directly discussing their own activity.

Acknowledgement

We first experienced this form of group dynamics during a two-day workshop with David Wasdell. He calls it 'matrix' work. At that workshop we spent one hour in a pair, one hour in a threesome and one hour in a full group of six. The same pattern was continued over the 16 hours of the workshop.

3.21 The quality of silence

Benefits
This is a chance for observation, reflection and sharing feelings. In a context in which great emphasis is generally placed on speaking, it is interesting to examine the positive aspects of silence.

Students
Intermediate to advanced; adults.

Time
15 – 20 minutes.

Preparation
None.

In class

1 Ask the students to pair up and sit opposite each other, observing each other silently for between two and five minutes. (Note: five minutes may seem like a very long time to look at someone else in silence, but our experience is that most people warm to this activity and it becomes increasingly interesting as time passes. However, if you feel this is too long, you can shorten the time, or ask students to simply sit in silence, rather than looking at each other.)

2 They then describe to their partner what they thought about and how they felt while they were doing this, before feeding back to the whole group.

Acknowledgement

We were introduced to this exercise by Dave King and Larry Cole on a Counselling in the Development of Learning course, at a time when the amount people spoke or didn't speak was becoming a block to the group's development.

3.22 Red herrings

Benefits
Explorations of how teachers deviate from their subject, and how students react.

Students
Elementary to advanced; teenagers and adults.

Time
20 – 30 minutes.

Preparation
None.

In class

1 Teach the expression *red herring*. Elicit/explain that this is a deviation from the subject in hand, something not relevant. If it is a class with several mother tongues among the students, ask each to put the equivalent term in their language on the board – get them to explain the way the term works in that language.

2 Tell them about a teacher you had who was prone to red herrings in class. Explain how you personally felt about these deviations from his/her lesson.

3 Ask the students to recall teachers they have had and to make a list, putting a cross by the names of the teacher(s) most prone to bringing in red herrings.

4 The students work in fours and compare notes on those of their teachers who frequently came up with red herrings. Ask them to evaluate whether the red herrings were useful or a waste of time – to what extent did the teacher come across differently while 'red herringing'? As an aid to their discussion, you could write up the following on the board:

> RED HERRINGS SHOW: spontaneity
> the real person of the teacher
> ego-tripping
> lack of respect for the students
> what students actually remember
> the teacher as a person

Follow-up

In this or a later class, lead a discussion on how we decide whether a theme is or is not a red herring. Ask the students if in your lessons, for example, there have been occasions when you have introduced red herrings.

3.23 Starting up

Benefits
Awareness of improved concentration levels and willingness to participate at the beginning of a class. Students are often not aware of how present or absent they are at the beginning of a lesson and are often at low energy. The activities here enable you and the students to check and develop concentration levels.

Students
Beginners to advanced; teenagers and adults.

Time
5 – 10 minutes.

Preparation
None.

In class

1 Organise your class into a standing circle. Stand in the circle yourself.

2 Clap your hands and pass the clap to the next student and so on round the circle back to you. Start the sequence again and then repeat until the clap passing is smooth to the ear.

3 Everybody holds hands in the circle. You squeeze and the next person squeezes the next hand. Do another round and another until there's a smooth 'electric current'.

4 Everybody breathes in and out three times in unison. You need to count them in and out (in 1, 2, 3, 4, hold, out 1, 2, 3, 4, etc.).

5 Ask the students to sit down again and silently answer the following questions as you dictate them:

- How do you feel now?
- How did you feel before?
- Which exercise suited me?
- How does the group feel?

Note that these exercises may also be used as energisers in the middle and at the end of lessons.

6 Ask the students to discuss their answers in pairs or small groups, or as a whole group.

3.24 Support partners

Benefits
Channelling students' classroom relationships into focusing on and helping with each other's language problems.

Students
Elementary to advanced; teenagers and adults.

Time
Ongoing, for occasional 15 – 20 minute slots in any lesson.

Preparation
None.

In class

1 Explain to the group that you would like to set up a system of 'Support Partners'. This means that during certain sessions, students will work in pairs to help each other with language problems, things they don't feel they've understood well or want to do more work on, or any issues which have become important to them.

2 Establish ground rules with the group, as follows:
   a) Students should choose someone who is not their best friend and, as far as possible, someone they don't know well or wouldn't normally work with.
   b) They should work in an atmosphere of uncritical acceptance, to facilitate change where necessary.
   c) Both members of a pair should ensure that they divide the time and space equally between them.

3 Get students to choose a partner with the above criteria in mind. (If you have an odd number, one group of three is OK.) Tell them to spend 15 – 20 minutes working together, as described above, discussing any problems they have had recently with their English, general areas of weakness or confusion etc. Monitor carefully and give help where necessary.

4 Repeat the process regularly in subsequent lessons.

Variation

Rather than pairs, students work together in ongoing support groups of three, four, or six.

Acknowledgement

We were introduced to the idea of Support Partners or 'Consultancy Pairs' by Dave King and Larry Cole on a Counselling in the Development of Learning course.

3.25 Where do I sit and why?

Benefits
Students become more aware of the classroom space and feelings about it.

Students
Elementary to advanced; teenagers and adults.

Time
25 – 30 minutes.

Preparation
Adapt the questionnaire below to fit the group/classroom in question. Make sufficient copies for each student to have one. This activity is not appropriate for classes in which the students do not have a choice about where they sit.

In class

1 Give out the questionnaire. Check that everyone understands everything. Students can either do it individually or interview a partner and fill in his/her responses.

2 Students then circulate their completed questionnaires for reading, or put them on the wall.

3 Finish with a feedback discussion, either with the whole group or in small groups.

QUESTIONNAIRE: Where do I sit and why?

1 Do you sit in the same place in class?
Always ☐   Whenever I can ☐
Usually ☐   Only by chance ☐

2 If there are only 2 seats left, do you sit next to a student you
know well or a student you don't know well? Do you sit next to
a student you like or don't like?

....

3 Which of these factors affect your choice? How do they affect it?
The teacher ....
Another student or other students ....
The board ....
The window ....
The door ....
Light ....
Warmth ....
Control ....
Safety ....
Mood ....
The weather ....
Type of lesson ....
Other? ....

4 Think about where other people sit. Is it related to their role or
position in the class in any way?

....

5 If the teacher asks you to move, how do you normally feel? What
does it depend on? If you are asked to choose a partner or a
group to work with, what factors affect your choice?

....

6 Consider spaces in which you often sit and have a choice of
where to sit – Sitting room? Kitchen table? Office? Other
classrooms? What kinds of factors affect your choice of where
to sit?

....

7 Make a list of possible benefits of sitting in different places.

....

3.26 What's on top

Benefits
This simple activity allows participants to clear their minds of distractions before starting a session. It is also a rich fluency/listening exercise and a chance to get to know each other better.

Students
Elementary to advanced; teenagers and adults.

Time
5 – 10 minutes.

Preparation
None.

In class

At the beginning of a lesson, students, in pairs, talk to each other for a set time about what's on top, i.e. what's uppermost in their minds. They should do this in 'counselling mode', in other words, one speaks without interruption while the other listens, and they swap only when they are told to do so. This pairwork may be followed by a group feedback session about what was said, how it was said, whether speaking was more difficult than listening, etc.

Acknowledgement

We were introduced to this exercise by Larry Cole and Dave King on a course in Counselling in the Development of Learning.

3.27 **What are you writing to?**

Benefits
The realisation of how we may project on to other people in the group.

Students
Elementary to advanced; teenagers and adults.

Time
40 – 60 minutes.

Preparation
None.

In class

1 Ask a student to come to the board and write down all the punctuation marks and accents used in English and in her mother tongue. She writes the signs and the terms for them in English, e.g.

!	exclamation mark	~	tilde
^	circumflex accent	;	semi-colon
*	asterisk	/	slash

The whole class helps the student at the board. Check that people are pronouncing the terms correctly.

2 Pair the students and then ask them to sit as far away as possible from their partners.

3 Ask each student to decide what part of the punctuation system his or her partner could be. Is Laura a comma, a colon, a question mark or a dash, for example? They should then write a letter to their partner in role as the chosen symbol, e.g.

Dear ! ... Dear Comma ... Dear Umlaut ...

4 When each person has finished their text they exchange letters with their partner and reply in writing. In their reply they write in role (the role chosen by the partner) but they write to their partner as she is, not in the role they chose for her.

5 Put people together in groups of six to discuss the experience and to share letters, if they feel comfortable doing so.
(You may want to take part in this exercise as a participant or you may prefer to move round the room offering help and support.)

Variation

If the students would prefer to go beyond the system of punctuation, ask them to brainstorm other systems at stage 1 above, e.g. the chemical elements and compounds, mathematical symbols (+ − % < > etc.), astrological signs, historical periods (Bronze Age, T'ang Dynasty, Renaissance, Tokugawa Period), etc ... The possibilities are endless.

Exemplification

Here are two of the letters that I got from students. The first is an opening letter, the second a reply to one I addressed to 'Dear Renaissance':

1 Dear Question Mark,

I think that for you the Give is not always very easy because you in your sentences always the questions.

It is very difficult to understand what do you think and what do you have in your mind. You are unforeseeable. I can never (prevenire) your actions.

I think these is a good thing. L.

2 Dear Mario,

Thanks for your kind letter, I like being praised by people. I know that I am magnificent by myself but it is always a pleasure when someone reminds me of this. Italy was a my cradle, from Italy I spread in other countries but my heart still remains there.

Yes, there is a relationship between me and Greece. There my forefathers were born and I cannot forget that, I cannot cut the knot that keeps us united. As for my younger brothers, it's the destiny of each important person to be copied so I don't mind as long as people can distinguish us – As for my step-brother, it's not my fault but my mother's –

Yours warmly,

Renaissance.

Acknowledgement

The device of writing a letter to your projection on to another person comes from ideas developed in Section 3 of *Letters,* Burbidge et al.

3.28 Who would you like to talk to?

Benefits
Breaking the ice. This can be the first step towards helping the group to gel.

Students
Elementary to advanced; teenagers and adults.

Time
15 – 20 minutes.

Preparation
None.

Note that some teachers and students may find this activity too threatening in a new group.

In class

1 Divide the group into groups of 10 – 12. Get the groups to sit in circles so that they can see the members of their own and of the other groups.

2 Tell the students to look around and to choose in their mind someone they would like to talk to, from any of the groups including their own, and to think about why.

3 Instead of asking them to talk to that person, get them to tell the rest of their group who they have chosen and why.

4 If appropriate, conduct a general, whole-group discussion at the end.

3.29 Yolks and whites

Benefits
Exploring feelings about the geometry of the classroom.

Students
Elementary to advanced; teenagers and adults.

Time
40 – 50 minutes.

Preparation
None.

Note

This activity uses and explores one of the most simple and elegant pair-work devices, in which an inner, outward-facing circle of people remains still while an outer, inward-facing circle rotates around them, pausing for brief conversations. It can be used in any situation where you want students to form and re-form pairs rapidly.

In class

1 Tell the students they are going to work for 15 minutes in two concentric circles, the inner one facing out and the outer one facing in:

(If you have movable seating, have them sitting – if not ask them to stand in two concentric circles either in an open space or in among the fixed seating.) Ask the students to choose which circle they feel like being in. Tell them the people in the outer circle will move round every five minutes while the inner people will stay put.

2 Once the students are in two circles (which need to have roughly equal numbers) ask them to talk to a person in the other circle about times when they have felt claustrophobic or shut in (e.g. in a cave, in the tube, in a lift). Ask them to think also of times when they have felt cosy and well-protected.

3 Tell the people in the outer circle to move two places to their right. Ask everyone to think of any sieges or naval blockades they have read about from history, e.g. the Siege of Troy, and to talk about this with their new partner from the other circle.

4 Tell the people in the outer circle to move round two places again and this time to discuss with their new partner the difference between living in the heart of a city, in the suburbs or in the open

countryside. Ask them to bring to mind people who live in these three different environments.

5 The students should now return to their normal places. Tell them, working alone, to write a diary entry about how they felt in their circle, and to decide if they would prefer to be part of the inner or outer group.

6 Outer people now get together and read each other's diary entries – inner group people do likewise.

7 Ask them to meet people from the other group and exchange impressions.

Alternative

Here are some other topics you might like to use for the talking points, especially if you have younger learners:

– situations in which you feel stuck and want to go outside (e.g. when you are ill, in class on a sunny day, detention as a form of punishment);
– situations when you are outside and would rather be in (e.g. when you have sports outside and it's raining/snowing, when you have to go for a walk, when you get lost).

4　The coursebook

4.1　Absent friend(s)

Benefits
Improved awareness of the coursebook through guessing about its author.

Students
Elementary to advanced; children, teenagers and adults.

Time
20 minutes; a further 20 minutes for the extension.

Preparation
None.

In class

1 Ask the students if they know the name of the writer(s) of their coursebook.

2 Ask the students to close their eyes for a moment and picture them. Make small groups and get them to talk about the person(s) they imagine – age, appearance, dress, where they live, type of house, what they like doing, etc.

3 Bring the class together and ask them to pool their imagined pictures of the author(s) (if you have an artist in the class they can do a sketch). Would the students like to meet them; what would they say to them?

Extension

If the students get into the activity and you have time try this follow-up:

1 Ask each student individually to write 6 or so questions they would like to ask the author(s).

2 Ask for a volunteer or volunteers to roleplay the author(s) and seat them at the front of the class.

3 The students then interview the 'author(s)'.

(See Empty Chair exercises by John Morgan in *The Recipe Book*, edited by Seth Lindstromberg for more on this type of roleplay.)

4.2 Students analyse their coursebook

Benefits
Students become more critically aware of coursebooks and, where possible, take some responsibility for choosing them.

Students
Intermediate to advanced; adults.

Time
1 – 2 hours.

Preparation
None.

In class

1 Brainstorm criteria for selecting a coursebook, e.g. reasonable price, good layout and pictures, fun to work with, interesting texts, opportunities to practise speaking and listening, clear grammar explanations, a varied approach. Put these on the board.

2 Ask the students in groups to discuss which of these criteria are important for them and, if they can, to rank them in order of importance.

3 Tell them to look at their own coursebook and award it a mark between 1 and 10 for each of the criteria they have selected.

4 In small groups, the students discuss the marks they have given. This may be followed by a feedback session in the whole group.

Follow-up

Where possible, i.e. in institutions where there are multiple copies of several coursebooks, when students are about to finish one coursebook and move on to another, prepare a grid with the criteria and space for coursebook titles. (See the example grid below.) Take in multiple copies of coursebooks for the next level up, as well as any 'extras' such as audio tapes, workbooks, Teacher's Book.

1 Give out copies of your grid and circulate the coursebooks. Ask the students, in groups of 3 or 4, to look at a number of coursebooks and award a mark between 1 and 10 for each criterion. Tell them to fill in their grid with coursebook titles and their marks.

2 As the students feed their results back to you, put the totals mark into a grid on the board.

3 Get the students to use the grid on the board to identify the book they, as a whole group, like best. If there are several candidates, let the supporters of each put forward arguments in favour of their choice, then put it to the vote.

EXAMPLE GRID

Coursebook titles:			
1 Price			
2 Layout			
3 Clear grammar			
4 Pictures			
5 Fun to work with			
6 Clear instructions			
7 Extras (tapes, video, workbook)			
8 Interesting texts			
9 Variety of approach			
10 Opportunities to practise speaking			

4.3   Analysing a coursebook unit

Benefits
Students become more critically aware of the coursebook and preview a language item in a subliminal way.

Students
Intermediate to advanced; adults.

Time
1 – 2 hours.

Preparation
Find a number of units in different coursebooks which purport to teach more or less the same thing at the same level (3 units would be enough if you don't have access to more). An item which you were thinking of teaching anyway, or something slightly below the students' level for revision purposes, would be suitable. Take in several copies of each coursebook or, if this is not possible, make photocopies of the relevant units.

In class

In groups, participants work on one of the units and consider the following:

1 the aims, as stated in the book;

2 how effectively they think these are achieved;

3 what – if anything – they would like to add or take out.

They then exchange their information with the rest of the class (probably the easiest way of doing this is to regroup, with one member of each original group in the new group), and choose the unit they like best.

You could then go on to use the unit to teach from, or you could leave it at that if you think the students have learnt enough from the analysis itself.

4.4 Book babies

Benefits
Checking expectations and motivation for a future course.

Students
Beginners to advanced; children, teenagers and adults.

Time
10 minutes in the first class, five minutes a day diary writing over two weeks, 30 minutes in class 2.

Preparation
This activity presupposes that you are doing a course which has a set syllabus or that you are working from a coursebook, and that the course extends over 3 months or more.

Note

This unit is used at the end of a course as preparation for the next course. You can use this activity in one of two situations:

– You are teaching the same group again the following course/term/year. You do this activity during the last two weeks of your present course.
– You are teaching a new class the following course. In this case you ask the permission of their present class teacher to work with them for a period.

In class 1

1 Give each student a copy of the coursebook/syllabus that the class will be following for next course/term/year. This should be done two weeks before the end of the course they are presently following.

2 Dictate the following instructions for the students. The dictated text will need to be simplified or translated for elementary students.

> – Look after your book for the next two weeks.
> – Take it home at night and bring it to school each day. Look at the book regularly to get a general feel for it, but you do not have to read it in any detail.
> – Keep a diary about your 'book baby'. Write something each day: a minimum of three lines and a maximum of a page. This can be in your language or English or a mixture.
> – The diary must be handed in at the end of the two weeks along with the book.

In class 2

Create small groups and have them exchange and read diaries. Round off with a whole-class discussion.

Rationale

The above activity gives each student a chance to assess how they feel about the next term. By focusing them on the future you are giving them a chance to come to terms with and increase their motivation for the coming course. The diaries and discussion will throw up useful feedback for you and them on how they see the language and the syllabus. This gives you a chance to fine-tune your practice and revise the content of the next course. In a situation where you have a choice of books, you may find you need to change the book.

The activity can also be done after the students have actually received a new coursebook but before they have really started to work on it.

4.5 Book fair

Benefits
Students become more aware of coursebook writers' thinking and take responsibility for materials used in class.

Students
Intermediate to advanced; young adults and adults.

Time
1 – 2 hours.

Preparation
When your students have finished, or nearly finished, their coursebook, find a number of different coursebooks at the next level up. If possible, take in multiple copies of these. Note that this activity is only suitable in situations in which students are able to choose their own coursebook.

In class

1 Brainstorm aspects of the coursebook, such as content, layout, methodology, clarity of instructions, illustrations, length/difficulty of reading/listening texts, variety. Check that students understand all these and put them on the board.

2 Students in groups of three or four take one book each and make notes under the above headings. This will probably take most of the lesson.

3 Each group then elects a publisher's representative, who sets up a stall at the fair to try to market their book. The rest of the students go round and gather information about each book. They should be prepared to ask awkward questions as well as easy ones, to challenge the ingenuity of the representative.

4 They then return to their original group to exchange information, before deciding as a whole group which book they would like to use.

4.6 Coursebook quiz

Benefits
Saying good-bye to the coursebook in an enjoyable and constructive way.

Students
Intermediate to advanced; children, teenagers and adults.

Time
50 – 60 minutes.

Preparation
None.

In class

1 When students have finished their coursebook, tell them they are going to compile an 'introductory quiz' for another group who are going to start using the same book soon.

2 Divide the students into groups, each in charge of a section (e.g. units 1–3) or an aspect (e.g. reading, grammar) of the book.

3 Tell each group to devise questions about their part of the book, which will help people new to the book to familiarise themselves with it, e.g. 'Does the book have a key? For what?' 'Are the tapescripts anywhere in the book? Where?' 'What is meant by "Language Focus" in this book?' 'What is included in "Exam practice"?'

   Groups should devise between 5 and 10 questions each, depending on the number of groups in the class. You probably need about 25 – 30 questions altogether.

4 Students circulate their questions to other groups and check for content and grammatical accuracy.

Follow-up

1 A volunteer offers to write up all the questions in neat, clear quiz-type form.

2 The quiz is presented to the other group, who use it in class before starting the new coursebook. They should be encouraged to give some feedback to the quiz compilers, perhaps in the form of a letter.

4.7 Humanising the coursebook

Benefits
Looking at personal reactions to the next coursebook unit.

Students
Elementary to advanced; children, teenagers and adults.

Time
40 – 50 minutes.

Preparation
None.

In class

1 Ask the students to go through the next unit in the coursebook picking out anything they individually find:

GOOD   BAD   INTERESTING

2 The students feed their ideas back to you and you start teaching the unit by picking up on one of their ideas.

In one secondary school class a boy picked out this sentence from a grammar transformation table: *My brother has more socks than I have.* For the boy, this was a remarkably bad sentence. The teacher decided to organise the whole unit (on comparatives) around sibling problems.

Acknowledgement

We learnt this technique from Hans Eberhardt Piepho, one of the major humanistic thinkers in EFL in the German-speaking world. Piepho acknowledges the influence of de Bono in the choice of categories in step 1.

4.8 Roleplay the coursebook

Benefits
This activity gives students the chance to look at the coursebook from a new angle, and provides light relief from using it in the standard way.

Students
Elementary to advanced; children, teenagers and adults.

Time
30 – 40 minutes.

Preparation
None.

In class

1 Just after finishing a coursebook, or when it is nearly finished, ask students to shout out the names of any characters who appear in the book. Write these names on the board, making sure that there are more characters than there are students. This is the 'Guest List'.

2 Students choose a character by taking turns to shout out a name. Rub out the names as they are chosen. (With a larger class, form two or three groups and ask one student in each to be in charge of this process.)

3 Students individually make a few biographical notes about their character, using what they can glean from the book and their imaginations. They then get to know their character better by introducing themselves in role to a partner.

4 Choose a host or hostess (or both) and explain that their role is to introduce as many people to each other as possible and keep things moving. They should, however, stay 'in character'. The students mingle and roleplay the situation of a party to which they have all been invited.

4.9 Self-accessing the coursebook

Benefits
Working with a finished coursebook gives students a chance to recycle what they have learnt from it in a creative context. It also provides an opportunity for them to say 'Good-bye' to the coursebook in a productive way.

Students
Intermediate to advanced; adults.

Time
2 – 3 hours.

Preparation
After finishing the coursebook, explain to the students that you would like them to exploit it for use as self-access material.

In class

1 Divide the class into small groups and assign different sections of the book to each group, e.g. Group 1: grammar practice exercises; Group 2: reading. Alternatively, students can choose the section they want to work on, and group themselves accordingly.

2 In their groups, students work on their part of the book, selecting from the material and either using the tasks set in the book or devising their own along similar lines.

3 They record on sheets of paper any book references and tasks to go with them.

4 Groups exchange their sheets of paper to check for mistakes/confusions and problems.

5 The book references and task sheets are put in a folder and kept alongside the book for use as self-access material.

4.10 Students teach each other

Benefits
Students take responsibility for planning lessons – and possibly teaching them. They become more aware of the thinking behind coursebooks and teachers' plans in the process.

Students
Intermediate to advanced; teenagers and adults.

Time
6 – 10 hours.

Preparation
Make enough copies of the worksheet and of the blank timetable for each student to have one. Prepare any 'extras' which go with the coursebook, e.g. cassettes, video, workbook (but not the Teacher's book) and bring them into class.

In class

1 Students choose a unit from the coursebook which they haven't yet done.

2 Give out the worksheet and blank timetable and make all the other materials (see above) available to the students.

3 Divide the students into small groups and get them to work through the tasks and take notes.

4 They will need to come together at intervals to form a consensus, e.g. after tasks 4 and 5. Task 6 should be done in the whole group. It's up to you how much autonomy you give the students in terms of how they do the task.

TIMETABLE

Date					
Time					

WORKSHEET

1 Skim through the unit. What do you think is the main aim? Are there any other aims (vocabulary, skills, phonology)?

2 What does the unit contain? Make separate lists in terms of:

Language work: grammar, vocabulary, pronunciation

Skills work: reading, listening, speaking, writing

'Learner Training', study skills: teaching you how to learn more effectively

Pictures, diagrams, etc.

3 Which parts of the unit would you like to use as students? Which would you not like to use? Why not?

4 Can you think of any materials or activities you could supplement this unit with? Could you bring them into class?

5 How long do you think the unit should take (including the supplementary activities)? When you have decided, plan a timetable for this period of time using the outline given. Try to make sure each lesson is balanced, interesting and fun.

6 Decide as a whole group how each part will be taught/learnt, i.e. either one or two students can take responsibility to 'teach' the rest (including preparation) or you can work together as a whole group or in smaller groups or pairs.

7 Do the unit, using your timetable and keep a record of how it goes (audio, video or notes).

© Cambridge University Press 1998

Note

Tasks 5, 6 and 7 can be used as an option if you see that students are responding well to the project. Otherwise you could take over at this point and teach the unit yourself, following your own timetable.

4.11 The wrong book at the wrong level

Benefits
Students become more aware of aspects of coursebooks which are not normally used explicitly as classroom material.

Students
Beginners to advanced; teenagers and adults.

Time
From 10 – 15 minutes to several lessons.

Preparation
Take in a set of coursebooks at the 'wrong' level for your class.

In class

1 With an intermediate to advanced class, hand out a set of beginners' books, and ask students to analyse the books for any of the following:
a) their content; methodology used; overall aims of each unit;
b) layout; design; pictures; tapes; workbook, etc.;
c) choice of topic in relation to target audience.

2 Students discuss whether, if they were an English teacher, they would use this book, or, if they were an editor, asked to produce a new edition, how they would improve it. This part can be done in the form of a roleplay or debate.

Variation 1

With beginners, use intermediate or advanced coursebooks as a source of visual material, and of texts 'above their level' but which they can read for gist or for specific information.

Variation 2

With intermediate or advanced classes, use beginners' or elementary books to analyse aspects such as 'cultural content' or the way in which gender, race and age are dealt with. Students list examples of the issue they are looking at, then categorise them in some way and use this as the basis for discussion.

5   Ways of learning

5.1   Four ways

Benefits
Exploring the four ways of learning, as proposed by Antoine de la Garanderie.

Students
Intermediate to advanced; children, teenagers and adults.

Time
50 – 60 minutes.

Preparation
Make one copy for every two students of the Four Ways sheet and one copy for every four students of the Swedish Story.

In class

1   Stick up copies of the Swedish Story (see below) along the wall of the corridor outside your classroom. You'll need about 8 copies for a class of 30.

2   Tell the students you want them to copy the story from the wall in the passage outside into their notebooks, but leaving the notebooks on their desks. They go out, read a bit of text, carry it back in their heads and write it down in the classroom. During this task watch the students as closely as you can, taking notes if necessary. This will help you in the next step of the lesson.

3   Ask 5 or 6 students exactly how they did the task, helping them from your own observation notes where appropriate to give as much detail as possible. Get them to focus on the sensory channels they used: some, for example, may have created a scene familiar to them, relating the story to their own lives; some may have 'photographed' bits of text and thus carried these mental images back to their notebook; others may have turned the story into oral text and carried it that way, as sounds.

4 Ask the class to form pairs and give each pair one copy of the Four Ways sheet. Tell them to read the sheet together and as they do so, to describe to each other their own way or ways of doing things in class (in language classes and other thinking activities). Do their ways correspond to any of la Garanderie's categories? (Some may find they use one way more than the others, some may report using all four pretty evenly.)

5 Bring the pairs together into groups of 4 or 6, to discuss in detail how they did the wall to table transcription. Ask them also to discuss how much they use these strategies in accomplishing other tasks.

A Swedish Story

Imagine the scene in the far North of Sweden: two lumberjacks at work in the deep forest. You can hear the ring of their axes for miles around. One is tall and thin and the other is stubby and fat.

The tall, thin one is at work, while the other one rests on his axe. Suddenly the tall lumberjack's axe slips and gashes his foot open: blood wells out of the toe of his boot. He turns to the fat one and says:

'Cutting trees can be a dangerous game.'

Oh, I forgot to tell you, this first part of the story took place in 1997.

And now on to the second part. The year is 1998: the same two men are in the same forest. This time the short fat one swings his axe, the axe slips and cuts his foot. Blood everywhere. He turns slowly to the other man, looks him in the eye and says: 'Yes!'

© Cambridge University Press 1998

Four Ways

The educationalist, Antoine de la Garanderie, says that his research shows four main ways people go about learning tasks:

Way 1: The learner tries to relate the material to be learnt to things he/she already knows. The learner fits the new into old schemes.

Way 2: The learner learns the new stuff by heart as a text. This can be done visually or auditorily: i.e. the learner sees the text in his/her mind's eye, or mentally hears it as a spoken text.

Way 3: The learner rationally analyses the new material, comparing and contrasting. This state of mind can also make the student challenge the teacher. People on the Way 3 track can sometimes annoy their teachers.

Way 4: Without conscious effort, the learner soaks up what is to be taken on board. Way 4 is probably how we learnt our mother tongue and most of the other things absorbed in early childhood. Suggestopaedia is unknown to most language students.

© Cambridge University Press 1998

5.2 Difficulties with listening: three cases

Benefits
Going beyond a purely linguistic frame in analysing individual problems.

Students
All levels; all ages.

When dealing with the language problems of individual students, it is often worth making an attempt to go beyond purely linguistic explanations for their difficulties. They may, for example, be choosing poor communication strategies, or inefficient learning strategies, or their problem may be simply physical, such as deafness.

Here are three cases in which the student's problem appeared to be one of 'listening comprehension':

Case 1

'When I have to go to an all-day meeting in English I can listen well for the first hour or so but after that I lose concentration. By the evening I just hear sounds.' (35-year-old manager in an international company with its HQ in the US. His mother tongue is Italian.)

I offered the following suggestions:

- Your anxiety to understand may be blocking your listening. Do a short relaxation exercise before your first bout of listening – allow the language to flow in. Make sure you take breaks during the day and do relaxation exercises in each break.
- Maybe you are straining too hard to get every word. If you concentrate on everything that is said you will soon fall behind the conversation and understand nothing. Listen for the key items, and trust your ability to guess the rest. (This is, after all, what native speakers do.)
- Switch off mentally now and again and let the sounds of English drift into the background. Very short, self-organised breaks are better than spontaneous mental absences.
- From time to time, sub-vocally echo the words of one of the speakers. As you do this, try to match your body position, breathing etc., to theirs. This will not only give you an insight into their form of words, but also their meanings and intentions. Soon you may find yourself accurately anticipating what the speaker is about to say.

Case 2

A 40-year-old Russian manager with upper-intermediate knowledge of English but lower-intermediate speaking and listening ability. In work situations with foreign delegates he relies on an interpreter. He says: 'When people speak to me in English, I don't understand.'

Every day, during the morning break, I questioned him fast and mercilessly about anything and everything under the sun. He spent 10 minutes answering a volley of questions like these: 'How long is the Dnieper? When did Beria die? How many windows do you have in your house? What sort of maternity leave do workers in your company get? What number bus do you catch home?' I tried to make the questions a kangaroo-jumping sequence, not a logical one. In this way he had to really listen hard to everything and not hope to guess his way to meaning from the overall context.

Case 3

A Brazilian economist on a lecture tour in the UK thought he needed to learn a lot more English, and came for one-to-one lessons.

My first reaction was: 'I can't improve this man's English in a dozen lessons over two months. Why does he want lessons?'

A brief interview revealed that his set-piece lectures went fine. The trouble came at question time. He felt he did not understand the questions. I give him a cassette recorder to tape his next post-lecture question session.

At our next meeting he played back the cassette: it was clear to both of us that he was not letting the questioner finish the question. He leapt in with the answer, regularly cutting the questioner short. He then admitted to me that he had a card-index in his mind of about 40 economic or political categories into which questions neatly fitted. If he heard a question he thought was coming from category 28, he immediately came in with stock answer 28. Working in English he would often miscategorise, and so give a brilliant answer to the wrong question and the wrong mindset. In so doing, he would frequently antagonise the questioner.

I suggested that he simply count slowly to three after hearing the end of the question. He tried this and our work together was over.

5.3 Modes of perception: 1

Benefits
Exploring general behaviour patterns linked with strength in either visual, auditory or kinaesthetic perception and thinking.

Students
Elementary to advanced; teenagers and adults.

Time
20 – 40 minutes.

Preparation
Steps 1 – 5: none; Step 6: prepare and copy for each student a sheet of short poems and rhymes.

In class

1 Tell the class you are going to read them a children's nursery rhyme in three different ways – they are to choose the reading they like best.

2 Go to the back of the classroom and ask the students to close their eyes. Stand very upright yourself, shoulders back and chin up and read the following rhyme or any other rhyme you know (or recite

it from memory) with as high a pitch as you can comfortably manage. (This voice quality is associated with listeners going strongly into visual mode – when they listen to this voice they tend to get more pictures.)

> Baa-baa black sheep
> Have you any wool?
>
> Yes Sir, Yes Sir,
> Three bags full.
>
> One for my master
> and one for my dame
> and one for the little boy
> who lives down the lane.

Ask the students to open their eyes.

3 Go to the front of the room, give the students good eye contact and say the rhyme with good change of pace, rhythm and pitch, making full use of your voice range (auditory mode).

4 Sit half on the teacher's desk, slump forward, go inside yourself and say the rhyme from the deeper part of your voice range, feeling it inside yourself (kinaesthetic mode).

5 Ask the students to discuss with the people near them which reading/saying they felt best with. Broaden out into plenary discussion and explain the three different voices you used: visual, auditory and kinaesthetic. The 'visual' voice tends to induce pictures, the auditory voice sensitises the listener to the world of sound, while the third, deep, resonant voice encourages feelings and movement in the listener.

6 If you have time, give out the sheets of short poems that you have prepared. (These could include nursery rhymes, nonsense poems, extracts from longer pieces; choose a mixture of lighter and more serious pieces, to give the students a real choice.)

7 Ask the students to sit together in groups of 3 – 4. Each student should select a poem from the sheet and read it aloud to the others in each of the three ways you have demonstrated.

Variations

1 Instead of preparing the poem sheets yourself, ask the students at the end of the previous lesson to bring favourite short poems (4 – 10 lines) to class. *Short and Sweet* by Alan Maley is a good source of short poems.)

2 Invite the students to try other ways of reading the poems, and to decide for themselves which way(s) seemed to encourage a) visual, b) auditory and c) kinaesthetic perceptions.

5.4 Modes of perception: 2

Benefits
Exploring general behaviour patterns linked with strength in either visual, auditory or kinaesthetic perception and thinking.

Students
Intermediate to advanced; teenagers and adults.

Time
30 – 40 minutes.

Preparation
Make a copy of the behaviour list for each student.

In class

1 Explain that though everybody perceives the world through their eyes, through their ears, and through touch and feeling, most of us are stronger in one or two of the three areas than in the other(s). Explain, too, that different learning characteristics may be associated with each mode.

Give the learners the behaviour list and ask them to scan through and see if they can think of three people they know, one of whom seems from their characteristics to be a typically visual person, one who seems more auditory and one who is strongly a feeling through the body or kinaesthetic person. Put the students in threes to compare the people they have chosen. (They are also likely to think of some people who have traits from all three columns.)

2 Ask each student to decide from the list whether they think they themselves are mainly V, A or K. Some may find they are a fair mix, while some may be heavily in one column.

	KINAESTHETIC	VISUAL	AUDITORY
RECALL	has an overall impression of what was experienced	remembers what was seen	remembers what was discussed, i.e. heard and said
CONVERSATION	laconic; tactile gestures and movements; uses action words	needs the whole picture; very detailed	talkative: loves discussions and may monopolise; likes red herrings; will tell a whole sequence
SPELLING	counts out letters with movements; checks with internal feelings	accurate: sees words; is only confused when the words are new	phonetic: spells with rhythmic movement
READING	likes books with a strong plot; reflects the action of the text with body movements when reading	excellent and fast; would rather read than be read to	enjoys reading aloud; reads slowly because he or she sub-vocalises a lot; good at learning / understanding new words
WRITING	thick, pressured hand-writing, not very good	neatness is important	talks better than he or she writes; likes to talk while writing
IMAGINATION	acts an image out – wants to 'walk through it'	vivid images; sees possibilities, details; good at long-term planning	hears sounds and voices
LEARNING	learns through touching and doing	needs an overview; cautious until everything is clear in his or her head; memorises in pictures	dialogues both internally and externally; tries alternatives orally first; memorises by steps, procedure, sequence; easily distracted
VOICE	chin down, voice deep and loud	chin up, high voice	agile in shifting pitch and tempo

Behaviour list, adapted from *Righting the Educational Conveyor Belt*, Michael Grinder

3 Explain to the class that it can often be very helpful in a conversation to try to match one's voice and language to the preferred 'mode of perception' of the person one is talking with. It is, for example, important in a teaching situation: a highly visual teacher is likely to get across best to his/her visual students and to use exercises that suit them rather than the auditory or kinaesthetic ones. A very kinaesthetic teacher may touch students a lot (within the norms of the local culture), which may not be appropriate for all of them. Ask them if they have noticed what your preferred mode of perception is, and to say if this may have affected (positively or negatively) their levels of energy and attention.

4 Explain to the class that one way of discovering whether a person is, at a given moment, in visual, auditory or kinaesthetic mode, is to observe their eye movements. Write the following table on the board (or have a poster ready), and tell them that, providing the person is right-handed, these eye movements (from the subject's point of view) normally indicate the following:

EYES UP LEFT	doing visual recall
EYES UP RIGHT	doing visual construction
EYES LEVEL LEFT	remembering sounds
EYES LEVEL RIGHT	constructing sounds
EYES DOWN LEFT	talking mentally to themselves
EYES DOWN RIGHT	deep in feeling

(For some left-handers the eye movement patterns are the same as for right-handers – for others the left-right polarity is reversed.)

5 Invite the students to find out for themselves whether the above correspondences hold by working in pairs and interviewing each other about, say, a recent holiday. Each time the interviewer sees a clear eye movement, she can ask a question like:

'Did you just get a picture?'

'Were you feeling something?'

'Were you talking to yourself?'

Note that steps 4 and 5 could also be done as an alternative or as a follow-up.

Acknowledgement

For more information on what Neuro-Linguistic Programming has to say about learning styles, see the Grinder book mentioned above.

5.5 Multiple intelligences

Benefits
Noticing one's own and others' ability within different 'intelligences'.

Students
Elementary to advanced; teenagers and adults.

Time
15 – 20 minutes during each of 9 lessons (not necessarily in successive lessons or in the order given).

Preparation
See individual lessons below.

Background

In his book *Frames of Mind*, Howard Gardner posits the first seven intelligences worked on below. The first five are widely recognised, though thinkers such as Piaget elevated the logical-mathematical one into *the* intelligence. To these, Gardner has added the intra- and interpersonal intelligences, which make a lot of intuitive sense to us as workers in the field of human relationships.

Gardner himself sees his theory as work in progress rather than a finished product. In fact, he has added naturalistic intelligence to his latest work – and combined musical and spatial intelligence into one. We have kept musical and spatial intelligence separate here and add metaphoric intelligence as a ninth form. And maybe you or your students could continue the list: might there not also be, for example:

• a religious intelligence?
• a physical survival intelligence?
• an accessing-the-unconscious intelligence?
• a cross-species intelligence?
• an altruistic intelligence?

The main use we have found for the theory of multiple intelligences has been to help us increase the variety of exercise types we offer our students. It makes patent sense to approach the student through areas where his or her strongest intelligences can be brought into play. The theory has also helped us to think much more broadly about our students' talents and their apparent blank areas.

Each of the nine activities that follow may be used on its own, or done in sequence (not necessarily in the order which we give) as part of a general exploration of the way people think and learn.

As an introduction to using any, or all, of them you might like to explain the idea of multiple intelligences to your students.

You might also conduct regular follow-up discussions on how they felt about each activity and when they felt a strong intelligence of theirs was engaged.

Acknowledgement

For more information on multiple intelligences see the Gardner book mentioned above and Gardner (1995) 'Reflections on multiple intelligences: Myths and messages in *Phi Delta Kappan*, 77, 200–209.

5.5.1 Lesson 1
Linguistic intelligence.

Preparation
Get three or four different native speakers to read the poem below on to cassette. Try to get male and female and/or young and old voices.

In class

1 Tell the class they are to listen to three voices reading part of an E.E. cummings love poem. Their task is to choose which of the three voices they like best.

> who knows if the moon's
> a balloon,coming out of a keen city
> in the sky—filled with pretty people?
> (and if you and i should
>
> get into it,if they
> should take me and take you into their balloon,
> why then
> we'd go up higher with all the pretty people
>
> than houses and steeples and clouds:
> go sailing
> away and away sailing into a keen
> city which nobody's ever visited,where
>
> always
>   it's
>   Spring)and everyone's
> in love and flowers pick themselves

2 Ask the students in fours to tell each other which voice they preferred and why.

3 Ask the students to write you a paragraph about what they liked or disliked about the exercise. Take in their papers for reading at home.

Students who like this exercise are likely to be people with good *linguistic* intelligence and probably also like the world of sound. It can be annoying to the *logical-mathematical* intelligence – what a wishy-washy task ... who cares about some silly poems and silly voices? Maybe you can get the language-intelligent people to lead the class in exercises involving stress, intonation, rhythm and word choice.

5.5.2 Lesson 2
Musical intelligence.

Preparation
None.

In class

1 Ask the students to leave their desks and stand wherever there is space in the room. Tell them they are going to close their eyes and

imagine they are a band leader, a choir master or a conductor: out there in front of them is the group of musicians they are leading.

2 Ask them to close their eyes and physically direct their musicians while hearing the music in their own ears. Give them around three minutes for this.

3 Put them in fours to tell one another what they heard and what they did mentally during the three minutes.

4 Ask the students who really enjoyed the exercise and heard and felt music to form one group. Ask the people who found the exercise difficult and pointless to form a second group. Ask the people in between to form a third group. Give them three minutes to exchange notes within their groups.

5 Ask them each to write a paragraph to you about how well or not they liked the exercise.

This exercise is really enthralling for some students and a complete turn-off for others. It gives you some way of gauging where the well-developed musical intelligences in the class are sitting. Musical homework, maybe, for them?

Acknowledgement

We learnt this one from Herbert Puchta, author of *Creative Grammar Practice* and *Teaching Teenagers*.

5.5.3 Lesson 3
Logical-mathematical intelligence.

Preparation
None.

In class

1 Ask the students to work out how many combinations of three fingers they can find on one hand (five fingers, counting the thumb as a finger). Make clear that 'combination' means three fingers in any order of counting, i.e.

> thumb + forefinger + middle finger

is the same combination as

> middle finger + thumb + forefinger

Give them a time limit of 7 minutes.

2 Let people give you any answers they can come up with. Do not confirm or reject. If anyone comes to you for the answer, tell them to wait until the end of the activity.

3 Stop the activity after 7 minutes and write the answer (10) on the board. Ask the students to write a paragraph describing how they felt doing the exercise and, if they were unable to find the right answer, how they felt when they were given it.

Acknowledgement

We learnt this activity from a Silent Way mathematician, Dick Tahta.

Other sources of exercise material

Students who show high logical-mathematical intelligence thrive on exercises like those in *Mind Matters*, Maley and Duff, and *Challenge to Think*, Berer et al.

5.5.4 Lesson 4
Spatial intelligence.

Preparation
None.

In class

1 Give the students the three figures below and ask them to check that they understand the instructions (e.g. the terms *identical* and *rotation*).

2 Ask them to work in pairs and take 10 minutes to carry out the instructions.

3 Ask them to write a paragraph on how baffling or enjoyable they found the exercise.

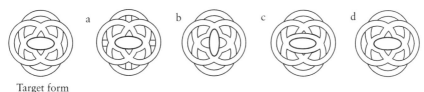

Target form

FIGURE 1
Instruction: From the array of four, choose that form that is identical to the target form.

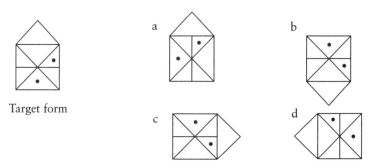

FIGURE 2
Instruction: From the array of four, choose that form which is a rotation of the target form.

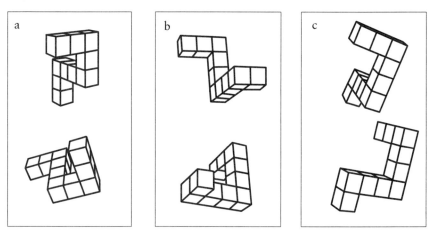

FIGURE 3
Instruction: (for *a*, *b*, *c*). Indicate whether the second form in each pair is a rotation of the first or is a different form.

Acknowledgement

Figures 1–3 are from *Frames of Mind*, Howard Gardner (Paladin 1983), pages 170–72.

Other sources of exercise material

There are some beautiful grammar practice activities for spatially intelligent people. Try Grammar Dominoes and Grammar Draughts (checkers) in *Grammar Games*, Rinvolucri, and Grammar Reversi in *More Grammar Games*, Davis and Rinvolucri. We suspect, though, that language teachers have yet to devise an adequate, broad battery of exercises that appeal to the spatial intelligence.

5.5.5 Lesson 5
Bodily kinaesthetic intelligence.

Preparation
Make a copy of the reading text for each student.

In class

1 Give the students the Marcel Marceau reading and ask them, as homework, to prepare to mime it accurately. Ask them to add their own ending.

2 In the next lesson, put them in groups of 6 and have each student produce his/her mime.

3 They write a paragraph describing their reaction to the activity.

Marcel Marceau reading

Our hero Bip hauls his suitcase on to the platform, climbs on board the train, locates a seat, and then, with considerable strain, heaves his heavy suitcase on to the overhead rack. As the train gathers speed, Bip is tossed about on his seat – his precariously rested suitcase falls out of the overhead rack. Bip manages to catch it and then carefully replaces it on the shelf. The ticket collector appears: Bip goes through his pockets with increasing frustration, turnsthem inside out, as all the while the train continues to toss him about. He becomes frantic – he goes through all the pockets of his suitcase ...

Please finish the story in mime, in your own way.

© Cambridge University Press 1998

Students in secondary school classes (and some adults too) desperately need to express themselves through movement. You will lift and motivate your kinaesthetically bright students if you give them body exercises such as listening to a story and acting out the protagonist's movements, or bodily representing grammar ideas (see the movement section in *More Grammar Games*, Davis and Rinvolucri), or doing three different walks before writing a letter from the viewpoint of one of the walkers (see Burbidge et al., *Letters*).

5.5.6 Lesson 6
Intrapersonal intelligence.

Preparation
Make one copy for each student of the questionnaire below.

In class

1 Ask your students to think about a trivial, annoying problem they have in their personal lives. Make clear that they will not be asked to speak to anybody about it. Tell them to shut their eyes and bring the problem to mind. Ask them to see the problem, to hear sounds connected with it and to fully feel the emotions connected with it. Ask them to talk to themselves in English about how they might solve the problem. This inner talking is done in complete silence for around 3 minutes.

2 Give the students this questionnaire to be handed back to you when they have finished:

QUESTIONNAIRE

1 How easy was it to be with yourself when you had your eyes shut just now?

2 How many solutions to your problem did you find?

3 Do you find that you do a lot of language learning work in your head, talking to yourself or others?

4 What sort of language work do you do in your head?

5 When do you think in English?

6 Have you ever dreamed in English?

7 How much did you enjoy trying to find solutions to your problem without reference to the people round you?

8 How much are you a loner?

9 Do you give yourself a good time when you are alone with yourself in your head?

© Cambridge University Press 1998

Some intrapersonally intelligent people may dread the instruction 'Now work in pairs'. One such person when asked to explain something in class said: 'Of course I understand this ... Do you want me to teach it to the others ...?' Chris Sion's *Talking to Yourself in English*, is a useful sourcebook for such people.

5.5.7 Lesson 7
Interpersonal intelligence.

Preparation
None.

In class

1 Ask the students to pair off. Ask one person from each pair to go outside for a moment.

2 Explain to the people left in the room that they are going to have a conversation with a partner about anything they want (except about the nature of this exercise) and to try and speak at the same tempo as the partner – so if their partner is a fast speaker they speak fast and if she is a slow speaker they speak slowly.

3 The people outside come back in to join their partners, and the conversations take place for about 4 minutes.

4 Let the people in the know explain the exercise to the others.

5 Ask each student to write about whether they think they are 'people people' or not. Do they enjoy thinking with another person, studying with another person, deciding things with another person. Collect in their papers.

Students with high interpersonal intelligence can be set joint homework, homework they can do on the phone. They will usually love 'humanistic' exercises but are less likely to be involved in less impersonal exercises such as gap fills or sentence transformations.

Variations

It is very easy to devise different rules for the 'insider' to follow in this kind of activity, for example:

- agree very emphatically with everything your partner says
- use a specified word in every utterance (fish, actually, myself)

- repeat or summarise everything your partner has just said before continuing
- match exactly your partner's body movements

5.5.8 Lesson 8
Metaphoric intelligence.

Preparation
None.

In class

1 Put these proverbial sayings up on the board, or choose your own:

- A bird in the hand is worth two in the bush.
- A stitch in time saves nine.
- People in glass houses shouldn't throw stones.
- Look before you leap.
- Necessity is the mother of invention.

2 Ask the students to work in pairs and to reverse each of the proverbs above, for example:

- Invention is the mother of necessity.

Ask them to decide, with their partner, what the new, reversed sayings may mean, if anything.

3 Ask them to write a paragraph about what sense they saw in the exercise.

Acknowledgement

John Morgan, co-author of *The Q Book*, taught us the proverb-reversing exercise.

5.5.9 Lesson 9
Naturalistic intelligence.

Preparation
None.

In class

1 Ask students to choose something they're crazy about: cars, a pop group, a sport or whatever.

2 Ask them to compile a top 10 in order of merit – makes of cars, songs by a pop group, teams or whatever is appropriate to their choice.

3 Have a brief exchange of lists in groups.

Rationale

We have added metaphoric intelligence, as in 5.5.8 above. Gardner has recently added naturalistic intelligence; Darwin had a strong desire to classify the world; young kids often know the names of all the dinosaurs.

6 Correction

6.1 Correction from eavesdropping

Benefits
Having natural conversations corrected and improved on.

Students
Elementary to advanced; teenagers and adults in multilingual classes.

Time
5 – 10 minutes.

Preparation
None.

In class

1 When students are talking to each other during breaks, note down any mistakes you happen to overhear.

2 Start your class from time to time with a 'correction slot' on such mistakes. Put them on the board and ask the class as a whole for improvements.

3 After you have done this exercise with a group for the first time, invite comments on what you have done, and allow any discussion that may follow: correction is a common source of misunderstanding between teacher and students and it is sometimes useful to let students express their feelings about it openly.

Variation

Collect student pre-class utterances and feed them back to them on a weekly basis.

6.2 Freeze-frame

Benefits
Concentrating attention on what's right and what's wrong in a problematic area.

Students
Beginners to advanced; children, teenagers and adults.

Time
A few seconds per intervention.

Preparation
Before a lesson, select a language area on which you want to make an impact. It's better to select an area to concentrate on rather than one specific minor problem. Have it in mind during the next lesson (or two) – the example below concentrates on grammar.

In class

When a student says something, whether right or wrong, that is within the area you have selected, 'freeze' the class. Repeat the original utterance. If you've stopped because the utterance was wrong give a correct version (but don't expect the student to repeat). If you've stopped because the utterance was right, simply repeat what the student said a second time.

Unfreeze the lesson and continue where you left off.

Example

One of us was teaching a class which had a persistent problem with the 3rd person singular 's' on the present simple.

STUDENT (during a game): She think it's very easy.
TEACHER: Stop! She thinks it's very easy. She thinks it's very easy.

The teacher then stepped back and let the game continue.
Later in the same game ...

STUDENT: He knows the answer.
TEACHER: Stop! He knows the answer. He knows the answer.

This technique highlights a problem area but insists equally on things the students get right as well as things the students get wrong. It is important to balance correction of mistakes with confirmation of correct utterances.

6.3   **Owning your own feedback**

Benefits
By *not* being specific about which student has which problem, the teacher makes the class more aware of the possibilities of self-assessment.

Students
Intermediate to advanced; teenagers and adults.

Time
30 – 45 minutes.

Preparation
Problem areas recorded on slips of paper: see below.

In class

1 While monitoring a speaking/listening or free writing activity, or a series of such activities, have some slips of paper handy. Use these to record any problem areas which you become aware of: write several slips for each problem area. These could include any of the following: grammar points, such as the present perfect or question forms; aspects of oral fluency, such as the ability to get a point across, the ability to deal with interruptions; aspects of coherence and cohesion such as the use of punctuation or linking sentences together; aspects of listening comprehension, such as the ability to cope with unknown words, the ability to ask for repetition when necessary; aspects of phonology such as rhythm or stress/intonation; non-verbal communication such as eye contact, hand gestures; even things like 'isms', e.g. racism, sexism.

2 After the activity or series of activities, spread the slips out on the floor and ask the participants to 'claim' any they think they 'own'. You should sit out as much as possible.

3 Ask students to discuss in pairs or small groups why they have claimed a particular slip, before conducting whole-group feedback.

Note that in a larger class you could write the problem areas on the board and ask the students to copy their own into their notebooks.

Variations

1 One variation is to be rather more concrete by writing on slips only things which you have already decided you want to focus on, if, for example, you know they are causing students some difficulty.

2 Use examples of mistakes rather than their definition, e.g. 'Have he been to New York?'; 'Johns car'; '/kʌmfəːteɪbl/'.

6.4 Possible or not, yes or no

Benefits
Students experience working from their own resources with their teacher acting as a technician not a parent or a priest. Student independence.

Students
Beginners to advanced; teenagers or adults.

Time
50 – 60 minutes.

Preparation
Prepare a list of 15–20 sentences which are possible and not possible in English: see below.

In class

1 The sentences should be a mixture of what it is possible to say in English (i.e. right grammatically and likely to be said by a native speaker) and not possible (wrong grammatically or right grammatically but unlikely to be spoken by a native speaker outside a very specific context). An example from a Russian native speaker: 'Do you have a mind to have some more?' This is grammatically correct but not used by native speakers, especially in the context of offering. The sentences can be selected from the students' homework or be ones jotted down by you during a speaking class.

2 Group the students in fours. Each group needs 12 tokens (coins, counters or Cuisenaire rods). All the groups should be in easy reach of the teacher:

3 Warn the students that you will read each sentence once and once only and it is their job to decide whether the sentence is possible or not. Read the first sentence and give them a minute in their groups to make the decision.

4 After the minute is up each group shouts out 'possible' or 'not possible'. Take a token from those groups which are right, give one to those that are wrong. The aim of the activity is for a group to end up with no tokens. (If this happens early in the game give them another 10 and do the accounting at the end.)

Do all this in silence.

5 If the sentence is possible go on to the next sentence with minimum discussion. If the sentence is not possible, wait for the student corrections and explanations, don't give the correct version, unless you have to.

6 Read the next sentence and so on keeping to the one minute time limit.

Token taking and giving rules:

- take a token for correct 'possibles' or 'not possibles' and give a token for incorrect ones

- when a student explains why the sentence is possible or not possible take a token

- if their explanation is unclear give a token

- if a student asks a question refer it back to whole group

- if it's a useless question or in pidjin English give a token

- take tokens for good language expression, give them for poor language expression

- give a token if they go into mother tongue

At the end of the hour students will often have strong reactions to this type of correction which you can sit back and listen to.

Rationale

This is a forcing awareness exercise from the Silent Way. Teacher silence forces the students to fall back on their own resources. The students understand that the teacher's refusal to provide easy answers gives them the chance to discover their own way of helping themselves and each other.

6.5   To praise or not to

Benefits
Dealing with feelings about two different styles of correction.

Students
Beginners to advanced; children, teenagers and adults.

Time
Short interventions.

Preparation
None.

Background

Here are two approaches to correction which you can try out with students and then conduct feedback on their reactions.

In class

Technique 1

When a student makes a mistake that you decide to correct, say 'No' in as neutral a way as possible. Then wait. If the student or another student tries to correct but still gets it wrong say 'No' again. If /when the student or another student corrects successfully say nothing and continue the lesson. If necessary feed in the minimum correct information in a neutral way, without asking the student to repeat, and then continue the lesson.

Rationale

The above offers an experiment in 'adult' correction. There is always a 'parental' temptation to say, 'Yes, good' when a weak student says anything. There is a temptation to say 'Not quite right' when it's more appropriate to say, 'No.' "Tea and sympathy" may be more damaging than straight, appropriate, unpatronising correction. Consistency of message is also important – you give students more equal treatment with this type of correction. Caleb Gattegno called this forcing awareness. Students quickly get used to this way of working. The essence of this technique is to do the minimum necessary.

Technique 2

When a student makes a mistake that you decide to correct, repeat the wrong utterance and wait. Prompt the student if necessary, and then praise any correct version you get. If no correction is forthcoming give a model, get the student to repeat and praise the correct repetition of the model.

After doing both techniques allow feedback time. A reflective chat with a colleague who has agreed to try the same experiment is worth having.

Rationale

Some of our reactions to experimenting with the above were:
Saying 'no' is an adult way of acting, for both the person who says it and the person who it's said to. Praise can be parental. Saying no is non-judgemental and neutral. It is a clear, technical and concrete way of showing the student that something is wrong. Implicit in praising is the idea that other times have been worse or other people have been worse, otherwise why praise?

But we've also found that:
Giving praise to the whole class at the end of a lesson works well for us. Giving praise to individual students works well when others are not about: at the end of a class, chance encounters in the corridor and during quiet moments in group work. Concreteness in praising is essential: 'You were saying I'M GOING not I GO for the future in that lesson,' is more concrete help to the student than saying 'Your grammar was better'.

In summary, the choice is between being an adult technician or a parental helper who praises. The above exercise gives a chance for the students to notice the effect of both on them.

Note that in technique 2 it has proved effective to 'anchor' praise with discreet touch.

6.6 **Students choose corrections**

Benefits
Raising students' awareness of correction techniques and letting them make choices about how and when they want to be corrected.

Students
Intermediate to advanced; teenagers and adults.

Time
50 – 60 minutes and ongoing.

Preparation
Make enough copies of the Correction Text for each student to have one. Also prepare a list of approaches to correction (see step 3 below), but this should only be used if students don't come up with much.

In class

1 Explain to the students that you are going to examine common attitudes to correction and their reactions to them, with a view to adopting a correction policy which suits each member of the group.

2 Give each student a Correction Text and tell them to read it. Ask a few questions to check comprehension.

3 Brainstorm other possible approaches to correction which are different from those described in the text and put them on the board. These can include: the teacher corrects every single mistake throughout the lesson; the teacher doesn't correct at all but records the whole session on tape and uses this for later analysis/correction etc.

4 In groups, students discuss the approaches to correction they came up with and draw some conclusions.

5 Conduct whole-group feedback and make notes on what the students tell you.

Below are a number of follow-up suggestions. You can do any or all of these in any order.

Variation 1

1 Ask the students to note down during a lesson what you correct and how you correct it.

2 Put the students in small groups to discuss
a) the effectiveness of each correction;

b) which they liked and which they didn't like.

3 Collect feedback from each group, either on paper or as a whole-group discussion. Keep a record of their comments for future reference.

Variation 2

1 Tell students you are going to conduct half the lesson with no correction at all and the other half with total correction (i.e. correcting every mistake made), regardless of the activity.

2 Ask them to consider their reactions to this while the lesson is in progress and allow time for feedback at the end.

3 Conduct whole-group feedback and record students' comments for future reference.

Variation 3

1 Ask students to choose, in a given lesson, the type of correction they want by
   a) reaching a consensus at the beginning of the lesson; or
   b) electing a 'correction monitor' who decides for the whole group; or
   c) using coloured cards or rods on their desk to indicate
      i) (e.g. green) 'I want to be corrected during this activity.'
      ii) (e.g. red) 'I don't want to be corrected.'

2 Again allow time for feedback at the end and record the results.

CORRECTION TEXT

You may have noticed that your teacher sometimes corrects you and at other times doesn't. Perhaps during an activity in which you are practising a piece of language in a restricted way, she corrects you a lot. She may use gestures or a facial expression or a single word to make you realise you have made a mistake, and she may ask you or another student to put it right, or else put it right herself. If you are doing a freer speaking activity, she might not correct you at all. Instead, she might note down some of your problems and deal with them at the end of the activity.

© Cambridge University Press 1998

6.7   Stick or twist homework

Benefits
Giving students a choice between re-working a piece of writing or writing on a new topic but with the tutor's help fresh in their minds.

Students
Elementary to advanced; teenagers and adults.

Time
Over five lessons.

Preparation
Prepare 4 or 5 essay titles or written tasks for your class. If they are preparing for an exam these could be essay titles from past papers.

In class

1 In the first lesson, write the titles on the board or dictate them to the class. Tell the students the number of words they should write and when you will collect the essays in for assessment. Explain to the students that they will have two options when the essays are marked and given back. Either they can move on to another title from the list and write a second essay or they can incorporate your correction and feedback and expand the first essay instead. (Students who choose the rewrite option are exclusively marked on the expanded rewrite. Students who choose to write a second essay get a final mark representing the average for the first and the second essay.)

2 Collect the essays in the next lesson.

3 Having corrected the essays and given them a provisional mark, give them out to the students in lesson 3. Show the students the original essay questions and if you like give them a few more.

   Remind them that they can re-submit the original essay as it is and write a second essay for a total mark or rewrite and expand the first one acting on your comments.

4 Collect the essays in lesson 4.

5 Give the essays back with a final mark in lesson 5.

Rationale

The students who do choose to rewrite and expand are given a chance to have a look at the process of their writing as they work from your feedback and correction. The students who consider and reject the rewrite option will often take your general comments on their first essay on board while writing the second one.

Acknowledgement

This technique is based on one suggested by Peter Grundy, author of *Beginners*.

6.8 Student-corrected homework

Benefits
Students use their own resources to correct mistakes independently of the teacher.

Students
Beginners to advanced; teenagers and adults.

Time
50 – 60 minutes.

Preparation
Wait a number of lessons until the students have done an amount of homework which you would expect to take about 30 minutes to correct in class. The homework needs to be reading comprehension, grammar and vocabulary exercises and controlled writing practice and needs to exclude extended free exercises such as composition.

In class

1 Find out which students have done all the homework, some of the homework, none of the homework, in as neutral a way as possible. Then divide the class into groups of about four. The groups should be like with like: groups of students who have done all the homework, groups who have done some and groups who haven't done any.

2 Give the students a time limit of, say, 30 – 45 minutes to correct their homework together. If there is a group who haven't done the homework, they do it; a group who have done some, correct what's there and do the rest. They are to discuss their answers and reach a decision on who is right in any dispute. Make it clear that you

won't be available for consultation until the end. If there's something they can't agree on they can make a note of it. Leave them to it – we usually go out of the room. In some schools with younger students it is a rule that the teacher is not allowed to leave the room during the lesson for, presumably, safety reasons, in which case sit quietly in a corner of the class. (If you stay in the class you may get students asking you questions – try not to get drawn in.)

3 After the allotted time bring the class together. Answer any questions they may have. Don't collect in the homework since by now all of the mistakes should have been cleared up. Make it clear that the next time you have enough homework the same system will operate.

Note

The first time one of us did this with a class we had quite a lot of questions to answer at the end; the second time very few and subsequently almost none. (It also seemed that the questions were more relevant and were things that the students had genuinely not 'got' rather than them checking things they already knew.) We've found this system gradually reduced the number of people who don't do their homework.

Variation

Ask the students to have their homework ready for collection. When you see it on their desks explain that they have 5 minutes to find and correct 5 mistakes each in their homework. Explain you won't answer any questions at this stage. When they've had their 5 minutes ask them how many mistakes they discovered. Collect in the homework and take and answer any general questions. Mark the homework in the normal way and give it back later.

The main exercise above may be a big jump for some classes. This alternative can be a 'developmental' activity to bridge the gap in student expectations and introduce them to the process described above.

6.9 **Total feedback**

Benefits
Making ingrained and unconscious working patterns apparent with a view to changing them.

Students
Beginners to advanced; children, teenagers and adults.

Time
20 – 30 minutes.

Preparation
Choose and photocopy a suitable multiple choice exercise.

In class

1 Pair students and give each pair a copy of a multiple choice exercise. Assuming the exercise has 4 choices of answer, select a symbol for each; e.g. A is a pen, B is a rubber, C is a book and D is a piece of paper. Each pair needs to have all 4 symbols out on the desk.

2 Ask the students to look at the first question. As each pair decides on their answer they pick up and hold the appropriate symbol. If everyone agrees on the right answer move on to the next question. If there is disagreement ask the students to reconsider for a further minute and change their symbol if they think it's necessary. Alternatively, ask them to discuss their answers as a group.

Variation

The technique can be done with other types of exercise, e.g. right/wrong, true/false, meaningful/iffy/meaningless.

Rationale

In this exercise the students are forced back on to their own collective resources and so we have found that much less teacher explanation than normal is necessary. This is a good exercise for mixed-ability classes and classes that have been together for a long time. In classes there is often a pattern of confident students answering first and expectations about who is usually right.

In this activity, answers are given visually not orally and so, in effect, everyone can answer and see each other's answer at the same time.

Both the teacher and the student can use this feedback to re-assess strengths and weaknesses and observe ingrained patterns of behaviour. When we have done this the results are often surprising; 'weak' students flourish, and sometimes 'strong' students flounder.

Acknowledgement

We learnt this exercise from Dick Edelstein.

7 Teacher to teacher

7.1 Blow your colleague's trumpet

Benefits
Learning about your own teaching by appreciating a colleague's success.

In the staffroom

If a colleague tells you about something good that happened to them in class or with an individual student, keep it in mind, and then, later, tell other people in the staffroom about it.

Alternatively, write about what the colleague told you in a teachers' magazine.

Rationale

EFL teachers are often irresponsibly humble – we simply do not value ourselves and other members of our profession reasonably and adequately. While it may be hard to blow your own trumpet, to blow someone else's is acceptable and good. It does them good and you too.

7.2 Change five things

Benefits
Dealing with conflict between two colleagues.

Time
30 – 60 minutes.

The following presupposes that a conflict has arisen between two people and that they have both expressed a desire to deal with it.

The two people in conflict choose you, a neutral person who they both trust. You have the choice of refusing to help. All three of you agree to respect confidentiality.

Fix a limited time for them to discuss the conflict in your presence. As far as possible they keep calm. Each person gets an approximately equal amount of time (if necessary by timing them), and concentrates on stating how they feel and what they think, rather than trying to demolish what the other person has been saying. You listen carefully and intervene only to clarify things you don't understand.

You then write five sentences about each person beginning:

I would be happier if ....

Each person gets a copy of their and the other's sentences.

Exemplification

The example below shows the third person's comments from using this exercise after an official appraisal which went badly wrong and where both participants agreed to a neutral observer. The names have been taken out to respect confidentiality.

I would be happier if...

Person A	Person B
1 realised recognition is not to be had for the asking	realised respect is not to be had for the asking
2 realised that he has recognition	realised that leadership involves a heartfelt commitment to the school
3 acknowledged that the workplace was steady rather than dynamic and that that had certain advantages	accepted that part of his job was to cope with what he saw as difficult colleagues
4 did not make wildly over-generalised criticisms	didn't make unsubstantiated allegations based on lack of information of life in the school
5 realised that he needs to broaden his range of experience	would think how person A could be 'used'

7.3 Creative listening, or: everyone has their own solution

Benefits
Getting people to suggest their own solutions to problems; dealing with conflict and discipline.

Students
Teenagers and adults.

Time
10 – 15 minutes.

Note

The procedure below is for when a perceived problem arises in class. The procedure can be used aggressively, and if you don't feel genuine goodwill and an ability to show empathy, respect and good listening to the other party, it probably won't work.

1 When a problem comes up, take the people or person concerned outside during a break or when the rest of the students are absorbed in an activity, or arrange to meet them at a fixed time.

2 When you meet them simply maintain a silence and wait for them to come up with their own solution (see the exemplifications below).

Rationale

The thinking behind this exercise is that most people have a better solution to their own problem and that the job of a teacher (or a colleague) is simply to help them to identify the problem. Assuming the problem identified is apparent, then the process usually goes in three stages as follows:

1 The person concerned makes excuses or denies the problem exists: 'Why me? It's unfair. It's not my fault. Everybody does it.'

2 They identify the problem: 'OK, I was late.'

3 They identify a solution: 'OK, I won't do it again.'

Exemplification 1

On the second day of an intensive course, two 17-year-old students came in 30 minutes late and stretched themselves out waiting for a reaction. In my experience of this situation general warnings and tellings off usually proved ineffective. I ignored them until a suitable stage in the lesson when all the students were involved in a task which did not require monitoring by the teacher.

I asked the students to step outside. My response was to say nothing although I did maintain eye contact; the problem was apparent. The students then had the space to make excuses; I maintained my silence. They eventually identified the problem as them coming in late and finally apologised and promised to modify their behaviour. To a remarkable extent this worked. They never came late again and this disciplinary effort at the beginning meant that the students were involved and enjoyed the rest of the course.

Exemplification 2

I was asked by a colleague to talk to a student whom she described as having been uncooperative and disruptive. He had shown, by not participating and by refusing to work with the other students, that he did not much like the class or his peers. I arranged a meeting with him after school, but on my way to the meeting I bumped into him going in the opposite direction. He explained that he did not see the need for a meeting since there was no problem – I had to insist on him accompanying me to a quiet office. Not a good start to the meeting.

I decided to say nothing . This startled the student. I said a few words but substantially kept my mouth shut while indicating as best I could with eye contact, body language and by saying 'I'm listening' that I was giving him attention. He spent about a minute complaining that I wasn't saying anything and then about a further two minutes complaining that all this was unnecessary since there wasn't really a problem. I just listened – I found it difficult to 'just' listen. He then paused and said he was a bit fed up. He then added that he supposed that he was being a bit anti-social but he had good reason for this and anyway he preferred to work alone. However, he thought he would make an effort to integrate more in class and build a few bridges.

> The conversation took less than 15 minutes during which I had hardly said anything. He had analysed the problem and come up with his own solution. His class teacher later told me that although far from perfect, his integration in the class was reasonably good from then on.

7.4 Displaced feedback

Benefits
Giving and getting feedback which is acted on.

Students
Any two classes you are teaching as part of your timetable; teenagers and adults.

Time
A few minutes reflection after the first lesson, the whole of a second lesson.

Background
This is a procedure for taking a piece of feedback from one class and acting on it with another, as a way of experimenting with change.

Preparation
'Save up' a manageable piece of feedback about yourself. It could be something a class has come up with incidentally or it could be from a formal feedback session with a class. Wait until you are teaching a different class from the one from which the feedback came. Before the class, spend a few minutes reflecting on the feedback from the first class.

In class

Go and do your lesson with the feedback from the other group fresh in your mind. At another time, assuming the implementation of the feedback is successful, it's worth going back to the original class and trying it with them too.

Variation 1

Ask a colleague to save up a manageable piece of feedback. It could be something they want to say to you or something from the class. Arrange to meet the colleague a few minutes before you are due to do a lesson with a different class from the one from which the feedback came. When you meet, your colleague should give you the feedback and both of you should spend a couple of minutes interpreting it. Go into your lesson with the feedback fresh on your mind.

Exemplification

The feedback I was given was a piece of paper from the whole class from a formal feedback session led by another teacher. It said, 'No, Paul.' With our knowledge of the class and our different teaching styles we interpreted it as meaning that the students found my instructions unclear, especially in the context of one recent lesson, and that they were not always sure of why they were doing an activity. I wasn't in the mood to reject the feedback and went into a different class as planned. I collected my thoughts and worked on giving clear instructions and giving a rather more teacher-centred lesson than I would usually have thought healthy. At the end of the lesson, I felt really pleased. I had experimented and taken a good look at my teaching style and the lesson had gone well.

I also went back to the original class and gave clearer and more teacher-centred lessons and developed a good relationship with them.

(P.S. Looking at the above sometime later I would say that there has been a slight but permanent shift in my style of teaching due to acting on this feedback.)

Rationale

You can choose to accept or reject the validity of the feedback. Sometimes feedback can be very hard to accept and to act on because it hurts. The procedure above won't stop you having strong feelings about the feedback. However, acting on it with a different 'neutral' class is a safer and more effective first step to checking and maybe changing your practice.

Variation 2

This technique can also be used with colleagues rather than classes. When a colleague gives you feedback about how you act, try changing how you act with other colleagues rather than the one from whom the feedback came.

Classroom application

Students work in groups of three, one speaking – about a given topic or photograph – one listening and one observing. The observer's job is to give the speaker a manageable chunk of feedback which can be acted on – eye contact, paraphrasing, voice range, etc. The feedback should contain at least one concrete example. The speaker and the observer then swap roles and repeat the task with the same listener. ('Spoken three-ways' p.56.) This exercise is good practice for the oral part of many exams.

7.5 Getting labelled

Benefits
Looking at projections past and present.

Group
In a teacher development group or teacher training group.

Time
10 minutes at the beginning of a session, 10 minutes at the end.

Preparation
None.

In the group

1 You and the group brainstorm names or phrases that they remember themselves and others being labelled with when they were at school. Ours included 'clever but lazy' and 'smartie pants'; others could be 'teacher's pet', 'class idiot', 'good at sport', 'class Romeo'.

2 Write them quickly on to sticky labels and distribute them arbitrarily. Try to ensure that no one gets one which is appropriate. (Alternatively, ask people to choose the least appropriate one for them.) The label is to be firmly stuck on the person where it is clearly visible.

3 Now run your planned session.

4 Ten minutes before the end of the time you ask the group members to say how they felt about being labelled and if they observed any difference in the way others treated them.

Note

People often react quite strongly to even this light way of raising the issue of labelling, so it is inadvisable to use people's actual labels unless you are sure the group can handle it. Be careful of a person who has the label 'disruptive', however mild-mannered they look!

Classroom application

For homework, ask the students to ask around family and friends for what their labels were. Back in class brainstorm – you enrich or translate their text. This has given the students a chance to think about the appropriateness of labelling. You could leave it there or initiate a brief discussion.

Acknowledgement

Rick Sheppard introduced us to this exercise.

7.6 Remembering names

Benefits
Becoming aware of how we unwittingly evaluate students.

Time
5 – 10 minutes plus later thinking time.

When you have had 5 to 10 lessons with a class do this introspective exercise:

- Leave pen and paper by your bed at night.
- Immediately on waking in the morning, before you are fully conscious, write down the names of all the students in your class. Try hard to get them all.
- Then compare your list with the class register.

Ask yourself:

- Are there any interesting omissions?
- Why did you remember in that particular order?
- Does the order correspond to anything?
- Any surprises?

7.7 **Sharing a class**

Benefits
Getting to know a colleague better, specifically when sharing classes (i.e. when 2 teachers are jointly responsible for one class and each teaches part of its programme).

Group
With a colleague group.

Time
45 – 60 minutes.

Preparation
Photocopy (after adapting if necessary) the questionnaire below – one copy per person.

In the teacher group

1 Do the following as a lead-in to the main activity:
   – Each person ranks other members of staff in order of how easy it is/would be to liaise (share a class) with them. Make it clear that their rankings are to be kept secret.
   – Ask them to consider the qualities which make it easy/difficult to liaise with others.
   – Ask them to form small groups to compare their findings, <u>without mentioning any names</u>.

2 Give out copies of your questionnaire. Ask each person to complete it in their heads and work individually. Give a time limit of, say, 15 minutes. Explain that anyone can mentally cross off any question they don't want to answer or add any they feel is missing.

3 When they've finished, ask them to choose a partner to discuss their thoughts with – it could be either the person they're sharing a class with at the moment or a trusted colleague.

The questionnaire below assumes one main teacher and one second teacher per class and deals with issues that were current in one workplace at one time and may have to be adapted for particular circumstances. It is also possible to get the group to come up with their own questionnaire. Do the lead-in, then give each person a few minutes to write questions individually before brainstorming the questions on to the board or OHP.

QUESTIONNAIRE on pair teaching

1 How long does it take to plan a week's lessons; do you change a lot when you implement the plan?

2 Do you prefer to teach two classes of the same level?

3 Would you like to team-teach (more)?

4 Do you consider your class a private place?

5 What gets you most angry when you are liaising?

6 How much time do you need to liaise?

7 Are you prepared to share materials and ideas?

8 Do you feel happy teaching from someone else's material?

9 Would you feel happier teaching one class for all of their time? Would your co-teacher feel happier?

10 Do you expect, and do you hear, voluntary feedback from your co-teacher on how well she thinks the class(es) are responding to you?

11 How do you know your teaching style and the other teacher's are similar or different?

12 How well do you cope with being paired with someone whose teaching style is different from yours?

13 Does your bias in favour of your own teaching style ever stop you seeing the good points in someone else's way?

14 Do you think as the main teacher you should tell your second teacher what to do with the class?

15 Do you expect your second teacher to come up with ideas as to what to do in your class?

16 How do you react when you are told what to do in someone else's class?

17 As a second teacher do you expect to be given an opportunity to volunteer your own materials/ideas to use with someone else's class?

18 Do you expect your pair teacher to:

    a) find the exact place on a tape
    b) clean the blackboard
    c) keep the register
    d) return dictionaries/books used in class
    e) [other] ....?

19 ....

20 ....

© Cambridge University Press 1998

Rationale

One of the most common informal situations where teachers come into contact with each other is liaison over shared classes. In most situations where we have worked, two, or possibly more, teachers are sharing a class and have to decide the programme and how to share it between them. The quality of the liaison between the teachers concerned is obviously important to both the teachers and the students. Often, since you may have been working with a colleague for a long time, it's difficult to change patterns of behaviour in you and in them. Liaison is a major opportunity for colleague-to-colleague feedback. What is negotiable? What needs clear definition?

Acknowledgement

Claire Brierly introduced us to this activity.

7.8 **Students love teachers**

Benefits
Expressing feelings about students to gain perspective, checking on paranoia levels.

Group
With a colleague group.

Time
40 – 50 minutes.

In the teacher group

1 Each teacher in the group focuses on a class they have known well for some time and writes the name of the student they get on least well with and the names of the five students they get on best with.

2 Each person in the group then gives an exaggerated roleplay of what they imagine their least sympathetic student says about them in the student canteen.

> I chose D. He 'said': Paul is really scruffy and disorganised. He doesn't speak very good English and he doesn't know grammar very well and spells words wrong. In Switzerland he wouldn't be allowed to be a teacher. He can't explain grammar properly and he treats us like children. He wastes a lot of time and comes late but he doesn't like it if we come late.

I improvised this to the group using D's body language and accent as much as possible.

3 Each teacher, working alone, now writes one sentence to summarise what each of their 5 'best', most sympathetic students might write about them.

I wrote:

> J: He teaches 'real' English.
> N: He's my age.
> M: He's like my husband and he understands.
> R: He leaves me alone when I've got personal worries.
> N2: He's funny and he lets me be quiet.

4 Everyone should now read their sentences to the group. They can elaborate, and be encouraged to elaborate, where appropriate.

Note
It can be easier to be negative than positive. This procedure allows for a balance between self-criticism and self-praise.

Classroom application
Ask the students to roleplay one time they've been criticised by or dismally failed to communicate with a native speaker and then 5 times they've been praised or have communicated successfully.

Acknowledgement
We learnt this exercise from a session of the Cambridge Teacher Development Group (see *One Group's Experience*, Rees Miller, unpublished manuscript).

7.9 Teacher mapping

Benefits
Gaining insight by comparing two teachers' perceptions of the same students.

Time
90 minutes.

In the staffroom

1 Arrange to meet a colleague who also teaches the class that you want to focus on. The fact that he or she may teach them another subject is all to the good.

2 Agree with your colleague before your meeting that each of you will individually choose about ten students to focus on. Criteria for choice could include your feeling that they are good students, bad students, marginal students, students you make brilliant contact with, or students you find it hard to make contact with at all.

3 As this will not be just another give-and-take staffroom conversation, you need to agree and to stick to these ground rules:
   – Keep the student under discussion as the focus of your attention. Try not to make the student simply a pretext for putting forward your own views (or complaints) about teaching, the system, politics and so on.

- When your colleague outlines her feelings about the students, listen without interruption, trying to take on board as fully as possible what she is saying. This will have most value for you when it is really different from what you would say. Try to give her full, non-evaluative attention.
- When you are speaking, your colleague also listens to you without internal or external interruption.
- Only after you have listened to her and she has listened to you, do you discuss what you have heard in a normal conversational way.

Notes

The frame here is a counselling one. Your aim is not so much to reach agreement with your colleague as to broaden your view of each student by taking your colleague's views on board. Where the two of you disagree, you may profitably find yourself questioning your own observation, value system and self-perception. In the same way, you should beware of using (apparent) agreement with your colleague to reinforce your own prejudices. Avoid becoming judgemental, and allowing the discussion to degenerate into mere staffroom gossip.

7.10 Time management 2

(See Time Management 1 in section 2 **Language and learning processes** on p.66.) This exercise also works well as a way of getting teachers to examine their use of time. The following categories should be used:

Own time

Time which is specifically yours to do what you want.

Self-maintenance

Includes, say, having a shower but also cooking for your family as routine. Basically all the things you have to do to maintain the fabric of your life, your friendships and your family relationships.

Paid time

All those things you do to maintain your work and relationships at work. Taking a colleague to the bar for a drink because you feel you're not getting on as well as you have been counts as paid time since you're doing it to maintain your working relationships even though you're not being specifically paid for that bit of work.

Variation

1 Write your usual plan for the next week's lessons and make a note of all the housekeeping/maintenance tasks you need to do in the workplace.

2 Rewrite the plan so that all the class work is condensed and finished by Thursday. Make sure you do all the other things you intend to do by the end of Thursday.

3 Use the fifth day to do all the things you've really wanted to do in class and all the other bits and pieces or just swan around.

One of us stumbled on this variation by accident. He was extremely busy and stressed one week. So much so that he literally didn't know what day it was and finished everything by Thursday. The 'extra' day was one of the most enjoyable and efficient working days he ever experienced.

Bibliography

Berer, Marge et al. 1982. *Challenge to Think*. Oxford University Press.

Burbidge, Nicky et al. 1996. *Letters*. Oxford University Press.

Davis, Paul and Rinvolucri, Mario. 1996. *The Confidence Book*. Longman.

de la Garanderie, Antoine. 1992. *Le Dialogue Pédagogique avec l'élève*. Bayard Editions.

Dufeu, Bernard. 1995. *Teaching Myself*. Oxford University Press. Original French language edition: *Sur Les Chemins d'un Pédagogie de l'Etre*. 1995. Self published. Obtainable from Rilkeallee 187, D 6500 Mainz 31.

Frank, Christine and Rinvolucri, Mario. 1987. *Grammar in Action Again*. Prentice Hall.

Gardner, Howard. 1983. *Frames of Mind*. Paladin.

Grinder, Michael. 1991. *Righting the Educational Conveyor Belt*. Metamorphous Press.

Grundy, Peter. 1994. *Beginners*. Oxford University Press.

Hadfield, Jill. 1994. *Classroom Dynamics*. Oxford University Press.

Horowitz and Young. 1991. *Language Anxiety*. Prentice Hall.

Lindstromberg, Seth. 1990. *The Recipe Book*. Longman.

Maley, Alan and Duff, Alan. 1979. *Mind Matters*. Cambridge University Press.

Morgan, John and Rinvolucri, Mario. 1988. *The Q Book*. Longman.

Morgan, John and Rinvolucri, Mario. 1984. *Once Upon a Time*. Cambridge University Press.

Moskowitz, Gertrude. 1972. *Caring and Sharing in the Foreign Language Classroom*. Newbury House.

Puchta, Herbert. 1993. *Teaching Teenagers*. Longman.

Puchta, Herbert. 1992. *Creative Grammar Practice*. Longman.

Rinvolucri, Mario. 1984. *Grammar Games*. Cambridge University Press.

Rinvolucri, Mario and Davis, Paul. 1995. *More Grammar Games*. Cambridge University Press.

Rogers, Carl. 1983. *Freedom to Learn for the 80's*. Charles E. Merrill.

Sion, Chris. 1994. *Talking to Yourself in English*. Desert Island Books.

Swan, Michael and Smith, Bernard. 1987. *Learner English*. Cambridge University Press.

Woodward, Tessa. 1992. *Models and Metaphors in Language Teacher Training*. Cambridge University Press.